T0311555

Reinventing Accounting and Finance Education

In a world of inequality, social upheaval and environmental devastation, business education urgently needs to adapt and change. The question is how and in what direction? Professor Atul K. Shah takes a virtue ethics approach, calling for education to be personal, holistic and profoundly moral and sustainable. Justifications for this approach are given and more importantly, practical ideas and approaches of how culture and ethics could be embraced to create a more ethical accounting and finance profession are demonstrated. These ideas are drawn from examples and tried case studies, and help to empower teachers and reflective academics to seek for new ways of transforming the minds and training of future generations. Unlike most accounting and finance textbooks, the approach is not formulaic, but motivational and engaging. It is a meditation that both students and teachers can benefit from.

Atul K. Shah, PhD (London School of Economics) ACA, is an accomplished writer, teacher and social entrepreneur who has led a range of global initiatives. He is author of *Jainism and Ethical Finance, Celebrating Diversity* and *The Politics of Financial Risk, Audit and Regulation: A Case Study of HBOS*. Presently he teaches at the University of Suffolk, UK.

Routledge Focus on Economics and Finance

The fields of economics are constantly expanding and evolving. This growth presents challenges for readers trying to keep up with the latest important insights. Routledge Focus on Economics and finance presents short books on the latest big topics, linking in with the most cutting-edge economics research.

Individually, each title in the series provides coverage of a key academic topic, whilst collectively the series forms a comprehensive collection across the whole spectrum of economics.

For a full list of titles in this series, please visit www.routledge.com/Routledge-Focus-on-Economics-and-Finance/book-series/RFEF

Reinventing Accounting and Finance Education

For a Caring, Inclusive
and Sustainable Planet

Atul K. Shah

Routledge
Taylor & Francis Group

LONDON AND NEW YORK

First published 2018
by Routledge
2 Park Square, Milton Park, Abingdon, Oxon OX14 4RN

and by Routledge
605 Third Avenue, New York, NY 10017

First issued in paperback 2021

Routledge is an imprint of the Taylor & Francis Group, an informa business

British Library Cataloguing-in-Publication Data
A catalogue record for this book is available from the British Library

Library of Congress Cataloging-in-Publication Data
A catalog record for this book has been requested

ISBN 13: 978-1-03-209627-8 (pbk)
ISBN 13: 978-1-138-04056-4 (hbk)

Typeset in Times New Roman
by Apex CoVantage, LLC

To all educators who want to shape a fair, peaceful and sustainable financial future for present and future generations.

Contents

Preface

The 2008 global financial crash transformed global economics and exposed a lot of shams and scandals in modern finance, which are still continuing today. Whilst the primary blame went to bankers and institutions and their greed and hubris, the theories and teaching of accounting and finance largely went under the radar. This book addresses the major transformations in accounting and finance education that are urgently needed to shape a more ethical, equal and sustainable world. This book was prompted by an article I wrote for *The Guardian*, and an email from Kristina Abbotts at Routledge got me to write a much longer version of my frustration with accounting and finance theory and training. I am truly grateful to her for the inspiration.

I have been an academic for more than 25 years and have enjoyed the research and teaching journey, all while trying to question, uncover and share, with a social and ethical conscience. I would like to thank the organisers of the education workshops hosted by the Institute of Chartered Accountants (ICAEW) in London and the highly original and creative Audit Futures workshops organised by Martin Martinoff at the ICAEW. I am also grateful to my students at University of Suffolk who participated in my ethical experiments in shaping a creative, ethical and sustainable financial future for everyone. Their questions and experiences helped shape some of the stories in this book. I am indebted to my friend and role model, Professor Prem Sikka, who inspired me on this journey as well as my mentor, Jim Harding. My Jain upbringing played a huge role in shaping my thinking and reflections on these themes, for which I am indebted to my mother, Savitaben, and father, the late Keshavji Rupshi Shah, and the beautiful community in Mombasa where I was born. I cannot name all of the school teachers and lecturers who inspired me in my life journey, but they each played a significant role in shaping my thinking and curiosity, for which I am very grateful.

Atul Shah
University of Suffolk Business School, UK

1 Sustainability, virtue and living ethics

We are living in very turbulent times. Inequality is increasing, multi-national businesses are growing in power and reach, jobs are disappearing, terrorism and wars cease to abate and animals and the environment are screaming in pain. Competition, which was supposed to bring efficiency and equality, has instead brought monopoly and unemployment. More fundamentally, there is a global crisis of morality, as virtuous living is being replaced by materialism. Not only species but also whole cultures and societies are being decimated by the sweeping tide of unequal capitalism. There has been growing concern about the role of business, its actions and influence on wider society and the environment, and the spread of greed, selfishness and individualism in daily life. There is also a growing rebellion against the content of business education, especially the neo-liberal theories and assumptions of economic science. Surprisingly, these changes have not affected the demand for business education, which has grown significantly and spread globally, and students are individually willing to pay hundreds of thousands of dollars for an MBA qualification. Often, business education is seen as a cash cow for the wider University, and within this, accounting and finance is seen as a cash cow for the business school. And the culture of the cash cow becomes one of milking, rather than of truth, fairness, justice and respect for all nature, including the cow. There is too little reflexivity about the culture, values and content of business education. Its significant power and influence demands such critique and enquiry.

When business education becomes a business, it should be no surprise that the criticism of business conduct, ethics and character becomes captured. How can the practitioners of greed also allow its critique and challenge? In fact, the academy often becomes a place where business actions are legitimated (Hopwood 2008) and where professors become consultants and advisers to corporations, exploiting the brand and title that the University gives them. The salary they earn or the job satisfaction of being a teacher and role model is not enough – even for them, maximising income becomes a priority. The truth that knowledge and wisdom are often inherited and beyond market trading or price is anathema to many. The very ethics of knowledge and education have become 'consumed'. In stark contrast, in many cultures of the world, there is a deep respect for knowledge and wisdom, and it is not seen as a tradeable commodity. However, rarely do these cultures have a say in the content of business education. Even at home, the business education they provide in these countries is westernised and very materialistic.

Economics, the very science from which modern accounting and finance draws upon, has been facing growing criticism and challenge (Chang 2010; Klein 2007; Daly and Cobb 1994; Ekins et al. 1992; Kay 2015; Graeber 2014; Hertz 2001; Korten 1995). It has shaped inequality, greed and materialism, influencing the widespread exploitation of nature and society. There is a global student rebellion against high finance and inequality (Chang and Aldred 2014; PCES 2014), symbolised by the Occupy movement, and it may not be long before a similar rebellion arises in accounting and finance, the children of economic science. Many argue that the core assumptions of economics are false, and instead of creating a utopia of equilibrium, equality and harmony, economics has been at the heart of the modern-day obsession with greed and aggression. It has given moral and intellectual legitimacy to selfishness, individualism and materialism. Markets, instead of helping to build trade and create opportunity, have increasingly become monopolised by big financial institutions and corporations that defraud public pensions, investment funds and even corporations and shareholders with complex financial jargon and products (Das 2011; Admati and Hellwig 2013; Kay 2015). Banks, which are supposed to be the servants to business, have now become its masters. Questions are being asked today about what it means to be a business professional, as both accounting and finance professionals occupy privileged roles in society and yet have lost a sense of public purpose or accountability (Hanlon 1994; West 2003). The banker, long admired for prudence, integrity and conservatism, has today lost his respect, is often seen as someone who cannot be trusted and is pre-occupied with fleecing his clients and customers rather than looking after their savings and investments. As professions fundamentally rely on special knowledge and skills for their status, any questions over this expertise go to the heart of what it is that distinguishes their members as professionals. Business values have corrupted professionalism.

Faith and culture are deeply entwined, and both are denied and ignored in the mainstream teachings of accounting and finance. Faith also is a space where ethics become alive and grounded in a real-world living context, making it an arena vital for the study of ethical business (Shah and Rankin 2017). In contrast, philosophy is by its nature abstract and technical, making it difficult to guide actual choices and transform behaviour. Faith communities are influential spaces and networks where ethical conduct is operationalised and sustained. Faith provides people with the experience of community and interdependence, and away from selfishness, individualism and greed. To exclude culture and belief entirely from the teaching of accounting and finance is in my opinion fraudulent. Whilst the European enlightenment may have influenced western history as the dawn of a new intellectual era, the Indian enlightenment predates it by thousands of years (Armstrong 2006) and yet is ignored by western finance and economics scholars.

Fundamentally, money is a cultural and social construct, not an objective material fact. When we examine the long cultural history of finance (Ferguson N. 2012; Finel-Honigman 2010; Graeber 2014), we find that all over the world, faith, trust and relationships were core to its foundation and efficient management. Politics and power also influenced outcomes of debt and repayment. Graeber looked at 5,000 years of world history in countries as diverse as China, India, Africa, Europe and North America to find that there were some very common themes running through the creation, borrowing and saving of money and wealth. He found that accounting pre-existed the creation of money, tax was often the initial motivator of coinage and currency, and mutuality and exchange were facilitated without compromising relationships and trust. Somehow, this history was broken in the last 50 years, when contracts, markets and professionals replaced the need for faith, relationships and trust. As a result, there was a breakdown in banking and finance, and economic crashes which had never before been seen or experienced became normalised. Similarly, Finel-Honigman (2010) exposes the highly cyclical and at times fraudulent history of finance in Europe and North America, where boom and bust was the norm, and money and power were deeply entwined. In India, Gandhi wrote about a trusteeship approach to business which is little known and very different from contemporary western thought (Balakrishnan et al. 2017). The fact that modern students of these subjects have no exposure to such histories means that they have little to learn from past experience and memory is being actively destroyed.

This book examines and critiques accounting and finance education from an empathy for social harmony and equality, and a respect for animals and nature. It assumes a reader who is reflective about his or her teaching practices and curriculum, and concerned about the wider world and its peace and sustainability. The ideas presented here go beyond critique to practical suggestions about how teaching methods and materials could be reformed to incorporate a holistic approach, where ethics and virtue play a central role. The approach adopted makes ethics and culture central to the teaching and not marginal or peripheral. It aims to be truly diverse and inclusive, recognising that more than 90% of the world's population is not Anglo-Saxon, yet teaching and research are dominated by the West. Cultural imperialism (Said 1994) is a profound problem which needs to be acknowledged and not denied or avoided. Cultural assumptions influence the theories that are propounded, and the effect of this is worse when a technical approach predominates, disguising the cultural pretexts. This chapter sets the background for this reform, justifying why such a reflection is urgently needed and the huge drawbacks of mainstream approaches to accounting and finance education. Chapter 2 then goes back to basics and explains why these are flawed and how they can be taught creatively and meaningfully. Chapter 3 gives practical examples of how the teaching materials and methods can be reformed to meet the present global crises head on and avoid reinforcing its frauds and failures. Finally, Chapter 4 highlights the benefits of such a reformed and transformative approach for both the teacher and the student and wider society.

There is significant emerging research and evidence which shows that for many large multi-national corporations and professional firms, fraud is today at the very heart of their actions, not their periphery or an exception to normality (Hightower 2004; Monbiot 2000; Klein 2007; Whyte and Wiegratz 2016; Shaxson 2012; Kay 2015; Das 2011). In their ambition to grow and expand, to make ever-rising profits and wealth, managers of large and influential businesses have turned to corruption, deceit and manipulation as a normal way of conduct and behaviour. People working inside these organisations have become selfish, opportunistic and anonymous, caring for their private rewards rather than the culture and impact that they have on their colleagues or on society. Business leadership has become profoundly hubristic, psychopathic and immoral (Bakan 2004; Hare 1996; Kets de Vries 2012).

Professional law and accounting firms have become very obliging, sometimes even actively encouraging this behaviour, as they weave their way around government laws and regulations to help exploit every loophole for private profits and gain (Mitchell and Sikka 2011; Shah 1996b, 2015b, 2016; Picciotto 2007). Very simple ideas like honesty, justice and independence have been totally corrupted by the temptations of private greed and power. Countries and legal systems have been unable to stop this behaviour, and there is little personal penalty or reprimand. The worst that can happen is a corporate fine, which comes from the corporate coffers, and at times is seen simply as a 'cost of doing business'. Some argue that the modern corporation and professional accounting and/or law firm are directly at war with morality (Mitchell and Sikka 2011; McBarnet and Whelan 1992, 1999; Picciotto 2007, 2015). Whilst relying on laws and morality for their legitimation, they actively undermine it through their actions, without fear, punishment or conscience. Instead of living under the rule of law, we seem to be ruled by lawyers. In the absence of ethics and a moral conscience, gaming the system becomes a norm. In the absence of an ethical approach and culture, business schools could be harbingers which teach students how to game the system rather than to follow rules and respect law and authority.

Underlying fraud and deception is a deliberate desire to deceive and misinform or miscalculate. After the 2008 crisis, analysis showed that whole organisations and systems acted fraudulently (McDonald and Robinson 2009; Fraser 2015; Cohan 2011; Das 2011; Tett 2010). Even the Big 4 global audit firms failed miserably in their role as professional inspectors and turned out to be highly compromised by the profits from consulting to financial institutions (Shah 2017; Sikka 2008). This raises questions about the role of knowledge and education in the design of organisational structures, and the ethics of the people involved in designing and managing them. We may also legitimately ask why it is that so many University academics from all over the world failed completely to warn about the impending frauds and crises (Arnold 2009). What were they doing? What made them distracted and removed from such a colossal failure? Were they corrupted and captured, or disengaged and uncaring? What are the adverse consequences for teachers and academics from wrong or bad knowledge, or even fraudulent teaching and research? Is there a deliberate strategy to confuse society with financial complexity so that intellectuals and professionals can retain power over them and profit from the advisory work? Academics are meant to be reflexive and self-critical, so this historic event should provoke a significant moral and intellectual crisis, but it hasn't, sadly. Just as the bankers escaped with no punishment, and sometimes with even more bonuses, there were no consequences for academics at all.

Just as fundamental questions are being asked about business, the same questions need to be asked about the content, methods and culture of business education (Shah 2016; McPhail and Walters 2009; Mele et al. 2016). The business school is a pure product of American culture and has been influenced mainly by the physical and mathematical sciences as opposed to the humanities (Kim 2013). In Europe, there has been more of a pluralist *bildung* approach where the emphasis is on developing the whole person. Whilst holistic education (whole people, context and systems approach) is being widely seen as the call of the hour in the field of education (Seto-Pamies and Papaoikonomou 2016), business teaching is still today quite far from understanding the very meaning of the word 'holistic'. Its factory-based approach to teaching generates fat profits for the business school, but in the process reduces the student to a powerless receiver of business formulae, rather than an active participant in the learning process. In many ways, its present trend is towards more and more specialisation, and so the parts are moving more and more away from the whole.

Similarly, business school research can often be very parochial and detached from the real world (Hopwood 2007, 2008; Arnold 2009). In accounting, due to the demands of professional accreditation, the degree programmes are getting jam packed and overloaded, so ethics can only come in as a sideline if at all. This defeats the very purpose, as the current global crises demand a highly responsible, ethical and accountable approach to business. In particular, the huge power of multi-national corporations is highly concerning and dominates the practice of both accounting and finance – the Big 4 audit and consultancy firms KPMG, EY, PWC and Deloitte are themselves multi-national. Discussing the technical subjects without acknowledging this power and influence is incomplete and misleading. Often this power is driven by a singular business logic which is antithetical to an ethical approach. This cannot be mitigated by nice words and training on ethics which ticks a box, but makes no difference whatsoever to changes in business character and conduct. An emerging literature on accounting and human rights is showing that there is a new push towards a humane accounting which could transform accounting practice and financial reporting (McPhail and Ferguson 2016). Business and human rights reporting may lead to changes in business exploitation of people and communities.

Serious questions are being asked about what it really 'means' to be an intellectual and an educator in the modern era. The very purpose of teaching and research need to be reflected upon – are we happy to serve power without questioning its truth or legitimacy? What ought to be our mission in life as educators given the present global crises? Edward Said provided a series of significant reflections on this theme in his BBC Reith lectures in 1993 (Said 1993). Examining the history of knowledge and the intellectual, the role of Universities in research and innovation, and the rise in the variety of experts and professionals in the modern era, Said came to some profound conclusions about what special role intellectuals can and must play. Here we highlight some of these findings and evaluate their implications for business education:

- The intellectual must not allow him/herself to be captured and controlled by powerful interests, be it corporate or otherwise. He/she must be free to speak truth to power, irrespective of the consequences. Hence courage is a key quality of the ideal intellectual.
- Specialisation has created a large cadre of 'narrow' technical experts who continue to furrow their chosen discipline, losing sight of the

wider picture and the consequences and impacts of their knowledge systems and content. For Said, academics must avoid 'belonging' to a profession or even a discipline. Intellectuals should be like an amateur, open to question anything and everything, and be willing not to be agreeable or respected.

- He was against *disciplonatory* and warned intellectuals not to close off their subject to outsiders and instead welcome wider dialogue and engagement.
- Objectivity is never guaranteed and easily compromised by power and politics, but we must not give up efforts to strive for objective truth.
- Ethics and morality are central to the pursuit of knowledge and should not be marginalised or ignored in our evaluation of truth claims. It, therefore, means that sincerity and integrity in the pursuit of truth are paramount.
- Disciplinary boundaries are not sacrosanct, and often become devoid of context, history, politics and morality. Interdisciplinary work should be encouraged and celebrated, rather than suppressed and avoided.
- We must resist systems of accreditation and evaluation from becoming overly influential and controlling of the content, theories and methods of research and dissemination.
- Conflicts of interest are rampant in modernity, and the intellectual must strive to be independent and stay independent.
- Business education is pregnant with such conflicts, and the intellectual must, therefore, be vigilant about being compromised or controlled by commercial interests and agendas. Consultancies and advisory roles may easily compromise objectivity, and lead to self-censorship whereby academics avoid critical research or pronouncements. This is very true in the American finance academy, where external consultancy is commonplace.
- According to Said, the medium is not the message and should not be mistaken as such. Where an idea or research discovery is published is much less important than the content of the research and the ethics of the researcher. Given that in both accounting and finance a significant amount of research is done in Universities, which are obsessed with journal publication and rankings and evaluation, this is a dire predicament. The medium has become the message today, sadly. Academic journals are read by very few people, and they are not open access and often expensive to access. It seems the modern academic intellectual has to compete harder and harder to reach an ever-narrower audience. Then we should not be surprised by the lack of impact of the research on wider society.

- Universities can provide a safe intellectual platform for the pursuit of research, but the output of academic research should not be dominated by status or ranking or reputation but by the ethics and courage of the researcher.
- Individualism and egotism must be kept at bay if one is keen to engage as an amateur and welcome challenge and critique.

Thus truth and ethics need to be at the core of professional education and not at the periphery. Speaking truth to power requires independence, courage, respect and tolerance. The implications of the aforementioned are very relevant to this topic. In most parts of the world, there is little if any tradition of academic research or training in accounting and finance. There is little resource and space for the accounting or finance teacher to be reflective and pursue independent research, or even develop and grow by raising questions and conducting local investigations and evidence gathering. As a result, teachers often end up as consumers of overseas research and knowledge, and, therefore, we should not be surprised that American or British textbooks dominate the curriculum of Universities and private colleges all over the world. Where such space and resource for research is available, it needs to be used carefully and not abused. The content of the research and education should aim to help improve human, social and environmental well-being, and alleviate injustice, suffering and expert exploitation or profiteering. Even professional bodies should not escape critique from intellectuals, and their education methods and techniques are very relevant to academic enquiry.

Holistic education requires the teaching of context as well as content (Holland and Albrecht 2013), an approach which needs to be interdisciplinary and explain the whole before focusing on the specific subject and its knowledge breakthroughs. It needs to engage with the whole student: his/her mind, body and spirit, not just his/her biological brains. It needs to encourage and inspire in the student a quest for wisdom beyond facts and formulae, and an ability to question and analyse wider truths which help inform their sense of meaning and purpose in life. Its foundation is ethical and social and environmental responsibility lie at the heart of it and not just at its margins. Such an approach has to include faith and belief as crucial moral influences on people and society, and cannot pretend that it does not exist or is irrelevant. Purpose and meaning become very important, encouraging education to move beyond means and processes to ethical development and maturity. Positivism, where there is a deliberate attempt to avoid moral judgements or priorities, has no place in holistic education, as our values influence our research whether we like it or not. There is an encouragement of virtuous living, where human life is seen as responsible and accountable to nature and society, and needs to be caring and compassionate. The character and conduct of the professor matter significantly and cannot be divorced from the content of their teaching and research.

There is a vast and growing literature on business ethics, evidenced by an increasing number of books, research monographs and academic journals. One of the most popular global textbooks in business ethics (Crane and Matten 2010) highlights sustainability and globalisation as key areas of concern for contemporary business practice. This shows that many academics are concerned about this subject area, and there is significant growth in teaching and research in the field. Both Corporate Social Responsibility and Sustainability have been major issues of concern, although the literature has been dominated primarily by western ethical philosophy, and generally is secular and acultural. Broadly speaking ethical business education research can be classed into two categories – theoretical, where it draws on particular philosophical ideas and applies them to the context of business, or empirical, where newly developed courses are analysed for student impact and feedback. There is relatively little on culture and faith, and the idea that morality is often embedded in living communities and business may play a key part of that morality for many faiths of the world, is not well understood or appreciated. The growth-based commercial culture of most business schools often contradicts the very principles of CSR and sustainability. In most business schools, business ethics is taught as a separate subject and rarely integrated into the whole curriculum as a central focus of education.

A global survey of the academic field of business ethics and scholars' perceptions on the most important issues (Holland and Albrecht 2013) revealed that the top-two concerns were the curriculum and the credibility, with a majority saying that their non-business ethics colleagues have a scornful attitude to the quality and rigour of the research and teaching. There was also a concern about how to teach ethics without preaching, and the limitations in integration with core business courses. In some regions, like Latin America, there seems to be virtually no teaching of business ethics at all – implying that the neo-liberal capitalist approach is uncritically endorsed as the only way to do business. Thus inside the business school, the teaching of business ethics is political and can provoke tensions with other disciplines and personal values and beliefs of senior academics. I would imagine finance academics to play a key role in this opposition, given the content of their research and teaching. Evidence suggests that they never even engage in such dialogues steeped in their technical worlds (Hopwood 2008). The majority of the respondents to the aforementioned survey came from the USA, where business ethics has to be a core part of the curriculum under Advance Collegiate Schools of Business (AACSB) accreditation rules.

The battle inside the business school about ethical education is truly shocking and cannot be ignored. It is also very likely that the outer world does not know anything about it. If they did, they would be asking very serious questions and perhaps even avoid business education altogether, or campaign for its transformation. The war lines are about power and territory and control of science and truth. In North America, the salaries of business professors are often in the hundreds of thousands of dollars, so rewards and money are also central to the ideological battles. Evidence of this battle suggests that the global realities of climate change, inequality and social upheaval are of little interest to most business academics. It's a job and a vocation, and a route to personal power and profit. There is nothing selfless about it.

Crane and Matten (2010, pp. 116–117) highlight major problems with the mainstream western approach to business ethics:

- Too abstract/reductionist
- Too objective and elitist
- Too rational and codified
- Too impersonal
- Too imperialist

They recognise an important place for subjective ethics where cultures, relationships and local contexts can influence behaviour and enable people and communities to apply their own interpretations. However, overall their book says very little about either faith or culture, in spite of the huge influences, these have on lived conduct and behaviour across the world. Of most interest is their acknowledgement that western ethics are too impersonal.

The literature on ethical finance is relatively sparse compared to the huge growth and influence of the finance discipline in terms of scholars, journals, courses and professional bodies. Somehow, even though the origins of economics were firmly grounded in ethics, ethics has today become detached. Current research on ethical finance is primarily from a western philosophical and neo-liberal perspective, apart from writings on Islamic finance. A common text on the subject (Boatright 1999) draws from ethical theory to analyse particular activities like financial services and financial markets. An accomplished and renowned Nobel laureate at Yale (Shiller 2012) makes a plea of concern about what has become of the world of finance, and what must change to build a good society. Shiller dissects the roles and responsibilities of professionals, and aspects of contemporary finance theory from a normative viewpoint, but avoids critiquing its fundamental assumptions, culture and ideology. He misses the key point that the very basis of finance theory is deeply problematic (McGoun and Zielonka

2006; Daly and Cobb 1994; Gendron and Smith-Lacroix 2013; Frankfurter and McGoun 2002).

The 2008 global financial crash has inspired a number of reports and books questioning the morality of finance (see e.g. Angelides et al. 2011; Tyrie et al. 2013; Das 2011; Santoro and Strauss 2013). Hendry (2013) develops and uses a philosophical framework of normative ethics to analyse core finance activities like lending and borrowing, or trading and speculation. None of these works take any explicit 'cultural' approach to ethical finance, or consider eastern philosophies on ethical finance. Sadly, there is little diversity of thought and theorising in finance (Gendron and Smith-Lacroix 2013). Faith ethics are virtually ignored by these studies, even when we know that faith has played a huge influence on the history of finance (Graeber 2014). Shah and Rankin (2017) elucidates the ethical finance culture of one of the oldest living faiths of the world, Jainism, which also happens to be one of the world's most successful business and finance communities.

Wachtel (1983) showed that the promotion of consumerism and materialism leads to loneliness and isolation, breaking down the social bonds and communities which are critical to human happiness and fulfilment. He was a psychologist and predicted the mental health crises that we have today inherited from the West. A debt-fuelled consumer culture lies at the heart of this mental breakdown. Like the credit card, finance has the effect of bringing temporary happiness and long-lasting pain, medicine which business schools may not feel comfortable discussing and debating in the profit-making classroom. There have also been many critics of the growth at all costs mentality and its serious cultural consequences. Like Daly and Cobb (1994), Hirsch (1976) showed that there are social limits to growth, and material growth undermines the social and trust fabric fundamental to the operation of democracy and free markets. If we are not careful, teaching business in this way all over the world could actively destroy the cultural fabric that exists in those countries. Reforming accounting and finance education is also key to cultural preservation – we are engaged in a moral crusade to preserve and conserve our communities and social fabric.

In the last three decades, there has been a growing divide between research and teaching, which has also become unhealthy. As an example, at the London School of Economics where I studied in the early 1980s, the faculty comprise many famous global experts. However, the composition of their undergraduate degree and its content has changed little in comparison to the research that is being done there. When teaching and research are separated, students do not get exposed to new ideas and thinking, and researchers become more and more disconnected from the real world, where the only dialogue they seek is with other academic scholars or journal editors. They can get cushioned from fundamental raw challenge to their values and assumptions, thereby distorting their theories. This does not bode well if the aim of education is to train future reflective professionals who are able to question and critique their teachers and the content of their subjects. This may also lead to a hierarchical academic culture, whereby researchers feel themselves to be above teachers, and students are more of a nuisance to be avoided than a future generation to be trained in responsible business and enterprise. Teachers often are role models, and the separation of research and teaching may not inspire the most reflective future professionals at a time when they are needed the most. It is plausible that in business, academics behave like the theories they espouse – cold, calculating profit-maximisers. It should not be a surprise then to find them uncaring about the content of their education.

There are some exceptions and scholars of compassion and repute who have regularly critiqued accounting and finance practice and tried to build a community and advance a discipline. There are also significant academic publishers and journals which have provided a space for academics to publish their research, although a majority of these did not originate from USA. Scholars like Prem Sikka, Yves Gendron, the late Anthony Hopwood, Christine Cooper, Trevor Hopper, Marilyn Neimark, Chris Humphries, Rob Gray, Jan Bebbington, Richard Laughlin, Jane Broadbent, Janette Rutterford, Jeffery Unerman, Lee Parker, Ken McPhail and David Cooper are all pioneers of this field. However, when we look at accounting courses and textbooks, very little of this critical thinking has come into mainstream teaching (McKernan 2011). Professional bodies provide accreditation to courses which can help students get exemptions toward professional qualification, giving them further return and reward for their educational investment. Unlike the United Kingdom, where professional training is also provided after graduation by private colleges. In the USA, CPA (certified public accountant) training is mainly provided through University undergraduate and master's programmes in accounting. Students who graduate with accounting and finance degrees can at the same time become part-qualified professional accountants or bankers in the United Kingdom.

This book is different in that it makes ethics the central focus for teaching accounting and finance, and draws upon a largely unknown but hugely relevant philosophical and cultural framework, that of the Jains, for its inspiration (Shah and Rankin 2017). The Jains are one of the oldest living cultures of the world and believe in the interdependence of all life, and *ahimsa* or non-violence to all living beings is their core philosophy. Personal character and conduct are key to the life of a teacher of *guru*, and we must be constantly reflective about our speech and actions.

In writing this book, I draw from 30 years of experience of teaching and researching *both* accounting and finance at various Universities in the

United Kingdom and North America, and participating in international workshops and conferences on accounting and finance. I have a PhD from the London School of Economics where both accounting and finance were in one department at that time, and I am also a member of the Institute of Chartered Accountants in England and Wales, having trained and qualified with KPMG in the United Kingdom in the 1980s. I bring together both my professional experience and my academic and research engagement experience. In addition, I also draw from my considerable experience of leadership at a grassroots community level within the global Jain diaspora, one of the oldest living cultures of the world. Over the years, I have developed creative approaches to ethics education for young people all over the world and organised and attended many international ethics conferences.

The Jains are also regarded as one of the world's best entrepreneurs and financiers, and have a several-thousand-year-old history and lived experience of sustained success in accounting and finance (Economist 2015). When one engages at the grassroots, one comes to understand the challenges and questions people raise about business and its conduct and character. Although grassroots work and engagement is demanding, it helps us to understand how people practice and experience business in their daily lives. Holistic approaches to education require us to see people as whole beings, with mind, body and spirit, and connected intimately to their families and communities. As Gentile (2011) has explained, we must give voice to values in our academic work. Other accounting scholars have similarly echoed the huge importance of ethical education (Arnold 2009; Lehman 2013; Gendron 2013; McKernan 2011; Molisa 2011), although finance scholars are relatively very silent on ethical matters.

The approach adopted in this book can be understood as 'virtuous professionalism' or 'virtue ethics' (Crane and Matten 2010; Lail et al. 2017). The present global circumstances require all of us to be virtuous, and if we wished to be called professional, then ethics has to be at the centre of our actions, not the periphery (Sikka et al. 1995). The educator plays a highly responsible role in society, and we wish to encourage academics to take this responsibility and proactively help build a sustainable society. If we place ethics at the centre, then not just our philosophy or behaviour should come into focus, but so too must we examine the content of what we are teaching and the impact it has on our students. We must be prepared to ultimately transform business behaviours towards ethical conduct and culture. This also means that business school research has to be influenced by these ethical priorities and as teachers and academics, we should also endeavour to become virtuous professionals. Not only is this book suggesting a transformation in the content of education, it is also advocating a transformation in academic conduct and behaviour.

In the arena of accounting, a large portion of the graduates tend to go on to qualify as professional accountants, and increasingly ethics is seen to be an important part of this training. In finance, many graduates may go on to work for large businesses or institutions, and the impact of their work can be enriched by good training in ethics. The literature has tended to emphasise a philosophical approach as opposed to a cultural approach in examining ethical conduct and implications. Trained in logic, scholars naturally gravitate to philosophy, although in truth, faith, upbringing and culture also play a big role in people's actions.

Research also shows that a genuinely holistic approach to business education requires not just a reform of the curriculum, but the entire values and culture of the business school and its attitude towards staff and students (Holland and Albrecht 2013; Seto-Pamies and Papaoikonomou 2016). The methods of teaching and assessment, the learning atmosphere and respect for minorities that is established, the design of the buildings and accommodation of nature, and an open engagement with wider business, society and the environment are key to this. Whilst there has been an increasing tendency in business towards specialisation, the subject of ethics can get lost in the milieu, and a sustainable approach demands that context and virtues are never forgotten.

This also means that the simple and profound wisdoms of the world need to be recalled and reinforced among the learning community. This is especially pertinent to accounting and finance, which have become very technical and specialised, and in the process have also restricted the scope for genuine ethical engagement and dialogue. An Australian study found that over 90% of banking and finance courses had no ethics components whatsoever (Oates and Dias 2016). As West (2015) showed, quants (as finance mathematicians are called) have lost any connection with ethical thought and frameworks and are 'morally detached'. They occupy highly authoritative positions inside banks and financial institutions. However, they are not made responsible and accountable, and the complexity of their models makes them very difficult to probe or question. To some extent, the same can apply to finance scholars and academics who apply complex maths and statistics, but cannot easily be questioned about the ethical assumptions behind the models. According to West (2015), it is the quants' moral duty to disclose their level of ethical engagement when their models are put into practice. The burden of proof lies on them, although in reality, they command much of the power and authority.

Living ethics are more important than learnt ethics, given the times we are in and the urgency of the global economic and environmental crisis. Social transformation comes from practice not theory, and at the very least, we must understand existing cultures and practices if we are to reform conduct. The separation of learning from living, something often done subconsciously in business education, is deeply problematic. It creates a mind-set of hypocrisy and recklessness, implying that students do not need to walk their talk, and words like sincerity and integrity lose all meaning. The general tendency in business education so far has been on learnt ethics, partly because these can be written about and published based on authoritative philosophers and their theories. Living ethics is much fuzzier and cannot be condensed into a formula or a textbook. It is open-ended and some would call it vague and is about transforming attitudes, not just thinking. We can debate and discuss ethical philosophy till the cows come home, but if we are to transform behaviour, we must engage with the inner beliefs and values of both students and teachers. This can be very difficult to practice, but is required of our time given the urgency of our global crises, including the vast financial crash we have just experienced.

In this book, we will show a variety of ways in which living ethics can be debated in the classroom and even examples and role models that can be studied to understand how conflicts and contradictions are resolved by real people in real life. The ideas in this book will also encourage scholars and teachers to review and reinforce their lived ethics and apply it in their teaching methods and student interactions. Neo-liberalism has tended to encourage privacy and individualism, where people are permitted to have their own morality, including those in responsible and leadership positions such as business executives or business scholars. However, the approach adopted in this book assumes that we can no longer afford to hide our values, nor to be acultural or neutral in business education. Transparency and openness about our living values are key to creating a sustainable business revolution (Hawken 1994; Elkington 1999; Ekins et al. 1992). Overall, both accounting and finance have become increasingly impersonal over the years, and there is an urgent need to re-personalise them and build sustainable social capital. This means less analysis and more reflexivity and meditation, tuning into the voices of the voiceless such as trees and animals.

Business education is predominated by big business in the content of the courses, the research and case studies discussed and even the theories applied. Even some business schools like Harvard or Stanford can be as big as multi-national corporations. Many argue that they have become highly 'corporatized' and ideological rather than scientific and critical (Harney and Dunne 2013; Gendron and Smith-Lacroix 2013). As we saw earlier, the business school as we know it today is largely a product and creation of American culture, embedding its assumptions of neo-liberalism, individualism and materialism. In Europe, there is more of an influence of humanities in the curriculum and teaching methods. However, there is a general assumption that business theories are independent of size, type or often even national cultural differences and a desire to develop general theories applicable to all businesses anywhere in the world. This is especially true for mainstream accounting and finance education.

Big business is deemed to be *successful* by its power, size and market share and therefore worthy of study and even emulation. Harney and Dunne (2013) demonstrate that in an era of extreme neo-liberalism, where there is externalisation of costs and extreme regulation of the sources of value, University research and teaching has become highly compromised. The teaching curriculum serves the interests of corporate power and control, and critical theories and discourse are only applied after the mainstream is taught – if done at all. Thus the wrong fundamentals are explained and defended first before any critique can be expressed. Business ethics education starts from an incorrect foundation.

The personal reflections of a multi-award winning accounting educator in the USA, and a former editor of the *Journal of Accounting Education*, are telling regarding the extent to which corporatism has crept into the mind-set of the professor (Stout 2016). He recalls with pride the dean of his business school once telling him that he is good value for money. Stout used to openly tell his students – if at any time you do not think you are getting value for money, please stop and question me. To him, education was centrally about giving financial return. The article says virtually nothing about the ethical content of his accounting teaching, but a lot about how he cares for his students and colleagues, and encourages and respects them. The cultural assumption of giving value for money is imbibed in Stout's psyche, something which is generic in the American capitalist mind-set. Somehow, he sees no contradiction between capitalist accounting and his 'care' for his staff and students. There is a cognitive dissonance between his actions and his teaching curriculum which Stout seems to be totally unaware of. Given the fact that the largest funding in accounting research and teaching in the World is in the USA, this attitude, if generic, shows we have a very long way to go to transform the deeply held commercial values of business schools, professors and textbooks. There is a crying need for leadership and transformation in the content and theories propagated in this educational approach.

There is ample evidence showing how the complex rules, systems and processes of big business make them highly identity-stressed and political workplaces, run by lots of middle-managers, where most people are a small cog in a big wheel (Korten 1995; Hertz 2001; Bakan 2004; Tett 2015). There is very little intimacy about or with anything, making them impersonal and transactional, where the best rule for survival or progression is to look after oneself rather than care for the organisation (Hawken 1994). In such situations, ethics often becomes a joke or a spin factory, and there is no clear sense of right and wrong. What is right is what survives or prevails, or what generates profits and meets sales or other financial targets (Froud et al. 2006). There are countless examples when targets have been manipulated to appease the bosses or avoid taxes and fuel corruption (Whyte and Wiegratz 2016; Picciotto 2015; Hightower 2004; Monbiot 2000; Klein 2007).

Scholars need to understand that for young undergraduate students without much experience of the world, big business can easily become bigly confusing and diminish their confidence in the subject area. They can get swamped by the jargon and complexity, and there is no intimacy in the way they understand the subject or relate to it. Passing a subject would then become a textbook exercise, rather than a subject they would have enjoyed and engaged with intimately. They may be able to relate to small business, or may even come from business families. If such examples are given, they may engage personally with the subject and bring their own experiences into the classroom. In the process, students may feel that their own perceptions and experiences are important for the whole class to draw upon and learn from. This can be very empowering for learners. At present, the generic approach to accounting and finance education seems very disempowering.

Also, there seems to be a general absence of any teacher training programmes in accounting and finance all over the world, despite the huge demand for quality educators. There are also hardly any research books *about* accounting and finance education, in spite of the huge number of books on accounting and finance. I could not find a single book where an ethical approach is central to accounting and finance education. There is an assumption that just because someone has an advanced professional qualification, like a PhD or a professional accounting certificate, they are automatically qualified to teach. The training is done through direct immersion – learning by doing. There also seems to be no mentoring systems for teachers and lecturers in how they teach and for improving their effectiveness.

One can view this as a profound cultural aversion to teaching, or something that is seen as irrelevant to knowledge advancement and dissemination. Inside Universities, academics are measured and promoted on the basis of their research performance (Hopwood 2008), with teaching merely a job that needs to be done. Such warped incentives have significantly affected behaviour and attitudes towards students and learners, making academics cold and impersonal, often uncaring about students and their futures. The practice of business education seems to be similar to the highly individualist and materialist theory of business – every one for themselves. This has profound implications for the future of the academy. If a PhD is regarded as training for future lecturers, then the proportion of ethics and education philosophy and techniques in these programmes is crucial. It seems that neither of these approaches is applied in both accounting and finance, where there has been a growing focus towards common standardised training in subjects like research methods, or theory, but not much by way of behaviour, culture and sustainability.

There are thousands of business schools all over the world, with rapid demand and growth in business education in Africa, Asia and emerging countries. At any one time, there would be at least 100 million students studying accounting and finance at some high school, college or professional level. The supply of teaching comes not only from Universities but also private colleges and professional education establishments, which are also rapidly growing and expanding. The general direction seems to be standardisation of the curriculum, and mass production – large class sizes. This also makes business education highly profitable as there are significant economies of scale and the costs of production are very low – in contrast teaching physical sciences requires laboratories, materials and equipment which can be very expensive.

Given this economic power, reach and shortage of skills, where job opportunities for lecturing are plentiful, and rewards can be very good or at least secure and stable, we should not be surprised by the 'crisis' in accounting education research (Rebele and St. Pierre 2015) and academic accounting and finance research (Hopwood 2007; Gendron and Smith-Lacroix 2013) which people are proclaiming. Like the bankers, we are not genuinely accountable for our behaviour, pedagogy and curriculum – our technical sophistication excludes the public from questioning the knowledge base. We use complexity to hide from view. Our power and status reduces our need for accountability or even connecting to the real world of financial practice. It seems accounting academics have made themselves unaccountable to society.

Both accounting and finance are core business subjects, central to any degree or business qualification. As an estimate, at any one time, there would be at least 100,000 teachers and lecturers in accounting and finance all over the world. Hence the content of this education is highly influential, and very worthy of critique and reflection, given the rapidly changing ecosystem we live in today. We must also not lose sight of the *historical context* of such education, which was virtually nowhere in terms of size, demand and influence even 50 years ago. Today, its impact on contemporary business conduct and behaviour, and therefore on national and global economies, is huge and growing. At a time when we are reflecting deeply on global inequality, climate change and financial and economic crises, the content of accounting and finance education and research becomes profoundly important. It has a very large and powerful footprint on the planet.

Tragically, the global rankings of research journals and business schools are having a hugely adverse effect on whole research traditions (Willmott

2011), with the American research becoming increasingly narrow and technocratic, and European research losing its diversity and interdisciplinary richness and with pressure intense in elite business schools to publish in top-ranked and therefore paradigmatically narrow journals (Hopwood 2008). In fact, in some Universities and business schools, there are significant battles between the economists and the psychologists or organisational theorists or accounting and finance departments are splitting up and not talking to one another. Similarly, research curiosity and conversation are disappearing and being replaced by a number of publications and journal rankings. The business school is becoming a place of infighting or pro-business research without creativity or social, environmental and political conscience. Being the pioneering editor of *Accounting, Organisations and Society*, Hopwood had a very good landscape view of the subject trajectories and its possible futures. Where there is no team within, how are such scholars going to be able to teach interdependence and sustainability with an ethical conscience? And if research is in such trouble, how will the knowledge base change to respond to the urgent global challenges?

Even in the field of accounting education research, there is significant stagnation and decadence (Rebele and St. Pierre 2015). The reasons they give are limited topics, similar research methods, same underlying theories and little creativity or diversity. The status of research in the field of accounting education is also very low – this means that those who conduct it are regarded as second-rate. Rebele and St. Pierre argue that in the USA, most accounting education programs still teach the same courses using the same, although heavier and more expensive, textbooks. Also in practice, it seems that a lot of teaching is being done by part-time professors, whilst the permanent ones are busy concentrating on trivial and narrow research agendas. Their evidence suggests that professors in accounting have no prior professional training and can come from other disciplines such as finance or economics. They have little to do with the world of practice. Hopwood (2008) explains that even at their massive American Accounting Association conferences where there are thousands of delegates, there are no displays of research books, only teaching texts.

As a result, many students end up getting inadvertently converted to the 'religion' of selfishness and greed that is glamourized and taught as science inside most business schools. This conversion comes not only from the theories and classes but also from the behaviour of their professors who generally do not make good role models, as they hate teaching. Those students who wish to probe the fundamentals and the ethics or assumptions which underlie the discipline are left without a language or method to raise those questions, as the techniques overwhelm the reflexivity that students can engage in. In my experience, technical complexity has the effect of

disempowering students and disabling them from genuine critique and challenge. This can suit the academic who wants to retain power and control,
and avoid ethical debate or reflexivity. Such academics often do not care
much about teaching anyway.

Incentives have a strong influence on behaviour. In business education,
most Universities and colleges all over the world are either private profit-
making organisations, or if publicly-owned, depend heavily on private sector
funding. There are very few places in the world where research in business
is publicly funded and therefore truly independent from business. In the
United Kingdom, there has been a long history of such research, but it is
now being increasingly compromised by a commercial and revenue dominated approach to education, with business schools often being forced to
be cash cows for the whole University. Public funding of both teaching and
research is disappearing. The idea of tenure or permanent contracts, where
academics are free to question authority and power, is also fast disappearing in many parts of the world. This leads to job insecurity and significant
internal competition, further perpetuating an individualistic culture.

As a result, there is a direct impact on the type of research done and
the degree of corporate critique and active public engagement by academics. This has an influence on the conduct and behaviour of academics both
inside and outside the University. Also, salaries are not very high, resulting
in fewer people attracted to teaching as compared to working in the private
commercial sector. As such, there are no bonuses for quality research or
engagement, and very close and continuous monitoring of research performance, measured by publication in globally renowned journals. This has
led to a tremendous sense of competition and a low attitude to risk taking
in research, and a significant disdain for teaching or other commitments.
Academics have allowed themselves to be silenced by research rankings
and external audits of their performance, and imbibed them in the way they
assess one another's research capabilities.

What many (Gendron 2013; Hopwood 2007; 2008; Hopper 2013; Gendron
and Smith-Lacroix 2013) have observed about the academy of accounting
and finance is that apart from a few notable exceptions, it has become individualistic. I fail to see a community of scholars, with a shared desire to
learn and advance a discipline – it is marked by independence, not interdependence. Young academics are left to fend for themselves to carve out their
own personal careers. Often the selfishness and individualism that is taught
in the theories and classrooms shapes the behaviour of academics, thereby
adversely influencing their students. I fail to see how a subject or set of disciplines can advance within such a culture. There are some people who have
developed a skill of writing journal articles in top journals and they are able
to survive the cruel competition, while a large majority of well-meaning

academics struggle even to get a foothold (Gendron 2013). Mentoring is much needed, but in very short supply (Hopper 2013).

Whilst in accounting there are several academic journals which are dedicated to the critique and analysis of education (*Issues in Accounting Education; Journal of Accounting Education; Accounting Education; the Accounting Educators Journal*), I could not find a single such journal in the vast discipline of finance – it seems totally unreflective of its education processes, methods and impact. This is selfishness at its most extreme. The culture and behaviour of the academy have a major impact on the method, content and approach to teaching and research. In evaluating accounting and finance education, we cannot avoid critically examining our own behaviours and attitudes to the discipline and the morality we practice.

Many are arguing that the pressures to publish or perish, and the power and dominance of elite journals, is engendering an increasingly insecure and competitive culture, which has serious long-term effects (Sikka et al. 1995; Willmott 2011; Hopper 2013; Harney and Dunne 2013; Hopwood 2007; Cooper et al. 2005). Knowledge production and dissemination are going very far from wisdoms like truth and purity, and the peer-review process has become a closed intellectual club where innovation and creativity are often stifled (Willmott 2011), and long-term research, which takes years to shape, is actively being discouraged by modern-day measurement and assessment systems. The methods of researcher accountability, are undermining the ethics, in the process removing research from pressing real-world crises, like the global financial crash, and the desperate need for creating a fair, sustainable, peaceful and healthy human society (Gendron 2013). The social scientist today is being forced to become part of a factory production line, and regularly needs to prove their 'intellectual' ability and status (Willmott 2011). This also makes the academy less critical and challenging of business, as they are busy convincing each other about how clever they are. Peers control recruitment and promotion decisions. Journal editors themselves compete for higher journal status, thereby making them also risk-averse to innovation and radical breakthroughs which could challenge existing paradigms. Their research impact factors are being closely monitored.

Despite huge volumes of research on the philosophy of education, and the role of Universities in public life, modern business textbooks are written in a way which virtually ignores these findings (see e.g. Deegan and Ward 2013; Brealey et al. 2014). They are ideological, formulaic and technical, and standardised for a worldwide audience (Ferguson et al. 2009). There is no cultural intelligence or sensitivity displayed whatsoever. With the rise of the internet, teachers are now given ready PowerPoints and lovely interactive audio-visual material from which they can teach, without the need for much preparation or personal thinking or creativity. Publishers of accounting and finance books actively push such classroom adoption of core textbooks as they are financially lucrative, and once lecturers adapt certain texts, they continue to recommend them in future years. It is possible that in the absence of formal teacher training, the global textbooks serve as *both* training material and teaching material for teachers and lecturers. The students are merely consumers in the production line. Yes, education has been reduced to the consumption experience. In the process, critique and reflexivity are severely compromised, something which Solomons proudly campaigned against in the 1960s (Zeff 1995).

If the textbook publishers can tap a global market, the returns from minimal investment are huge. They have mastered the art of profit maximisation, where education, ethics and knowledge enhancement, are subsidiary to the process of mass marketing. So the income stream from publishing can become regular with little ongoing costs. When lecturers adopt core texts, they are in effect accepting a bribe from the publishers which makes their lives easy. Universities collude in this as the teaching of business, and in particular accounting and finance is hugely profitable. The larger the class size, the greater the economies of scale and profits that can be earned. Even though global accounting and finance research and education might not be supplied by a giant multi-national corporation, the reach and impact are as if it were highly standardised and manufactured.

There is also evidence of the rise and advancement of what Daly and Cobb (1994) call 'disciplonatory' – the worship of abstract disciplines as if they were true and scientific on their own terms. According to them, economics is the worst culprit of advanced abstraction, so much so that academics have lost the connection with the real world and are happy and comfortable in their theoretical abstractions (see also Kay 2011; Chang and Aldred 2014; Donaldson 1984). As the discipline gets challenged, they retreat more and more into these abstractions.

The relatively younger modern discipline of finance also falls into this domain. Its top-rated journals are virtually impossible to read and digest (Frankfurter and McGoun 2002; Gendron and Smith-Lacroix 2013) even by experienced finance practitioners, academics, lecturers or accountants including me. Given the massive failures of economic theory, the mother of finance is in trouble and accounting is also shaky given that its mother is finance. Accounting is often seen as the grandchild of economics. None of this has threatened the jobs of the academics or the power and authority held by these journals – the discipline remains highly colonised by tradition and abstract theory. Somehow, however, the research production line continues unabated, and we still have thousands of business schools all over the world promoting this highly damaging science and knowledge without any health warnings.

One critical aspect of this abstraction is the self-referential nature of modern-day accounting and finance (Hopwood 2008; McGoun 1997; Frankfurter and McGoun 2002). Hopwood (2007) laments that even the research has become self-referential, with academics increasingly talking to each other rather than engaging with the wider world. In its essence, money is self-referential – its value depends on what society and the economy accepts for its price at any given time. For example, even after decades of research in these areas, we still cannot theoretically predict the absolute value of a share, only its relative value. Similarly, even market prices are not objective or sacrosanct and can change dramatically very quickly as a result of myth, rumour or a herd mentality. Money itself changes value, so how can prices be truly objective? Given that accounting relies upon the objective reality of money in its calculations and measurements, its foundations are also very shaky.

The balance sheet is a hotchpotch of historical cost, market value, estimated market price, net book value, provisional gains and losses – there is no consistency, and often the outcomes of what passes as accounting is a result of political compromise as opposed to sound theory. Journals like *Critical Perspectives on Accounting, Accounting, Organisations and Society* and *Accounting, Auditing and Accountability Journal* regularly publish high quality articles which demonstrate the fundamental contradictions and paradoxes of accounting. Ideas like true and fair have lost all connection with what is ordinarily meant by true and fair – and even professionals who express judgement based on these principles simply follow the rule book, often helping their clients to bend them to their advantage (McBarnet and Whelan 1992; Shah 1996b; Shah 2015b). The findings of critical accounting research have not really permeated into the undergraduate curriculum, partly because of the professional bodies influence on the content of this education (Hopper 2013). The University is becoming more of a learning factory and less of a place where critique, analysis and judgement are developed as Solomons had anticipated (Zeff 1995).

For a majority of scientists, however, admitting their subjectivities and assumptions can be very difficult, as they have built their entire careers on it, so they carry on building the tower of babel, even when the foundations are very weak. Many have become deeply institutionalised and are very insecure without even realising or admitting it. The technical complexity becomes an important hiding place and protection. Asking fundamental questions may be seen as a challenge to their scientific authority and wisdom, so this is best denied or avoided. Similarly, the textbooks would primarily convey technical standards and accounting processes, and may mention this research as an aside, but not really engage with it.

One of the qualities we urgently need in the world today is reflexivity – the ability to quietly consider different ideas and facts, assimilate them and come to an honest view or judgement about truth and fairness (Molisa 2011; Hopper 2013; West 2003). This requires much more than technical skill or scientific prowess – it requires silence, patience and quiet contemplation, something I would call a soulful dialogue. In the world of business education, and the constant desire to perform and generate results and outputs, whether it be in terms of student numbers or pass rates, quality publications or awards and recognition, reflexivity is under threat.

If we truly understand nature and how it operates, the steadfastness and silence of a tree for example, then we must learn to be reflexive and to widen this spirit in the classroom as well as the workplace. In time, reflexivity can bring a deeper inner self-confidence which no one can take away from a person. It can lead to discussion about ideas and policies, not just papers and credentials. Reflexivity can really help shape rounded and talented professionals who can provide impartial advice and counsel to a diverse range of clients and organisations. Sustainable finance cannot be achieved without a reflexive nature, character and mind-set. Future generations require us to be patient in our thinking and actions.

In charting a new course for accounting and finance education, it is important to understand its historical context. The first and oldest professional bodies in accounting, the Institute of Chartered Accountants of Scotland and the Institute of Chartered Accountants in England and Wales were founded in the late nineteenth century, at a time when accounting was not even taught or researched in any University anywhere in the world. It was a practice and profession long before it became a subject for research and analysis (West 2003). The first professorship in accounting was established at the London School of Economics in 1953, and at old and elite Universities like Oxford or Cambridge, such positions were not initiated until the late 1990s when their business schools were first established. Similarly, the history of finance education at University is even much shorter than accounting, with the first positions starting in the late 1970s in America. There was a significant growth thereafter, synonymous with the creation and expansion of business schools all over the world (Mackenzie 2006). The type and content of finance education and research, therefore, became strongly dominated by British or American culture and economic theories, to which the rest of the world became consumers and followers.

In a unique special issue reflection on accounting education by the journal *Critical Perspectives on Accounting*, Hopper (2013) acknowledges that accounting education in the United Kingdom is in need of reform, due to the rise in student demand for, and influence of, professional accreditation. He also laments the separation of teaching and research with low status accorded to research in education or teachers who do not engage in research. He expresses concern about the lack of professional bodies and accounting firms' engagement with University research, in spite of significant achievements and breakthroughs. Hopper is also concerned about the difference between elite research-oriented Universities and those which do not do any research. This two-tier system has significant implications for ethical teaching and a curriculum which engages with the flaws and limits of accounting. Large class sizes and the focus on commercialisation are things that he finds deeply disturbing if we are to encourage critical and reflective thinking.

As compared to human history on the planet, the history of accounting or finance education and research is virtually negligible, in spite of the huge impact it has on the planet and its social and eco-systems. It is merely an infant, but one which has very quickly come to have vast influence on the planet. West (2003) argues that accounting does not deserve to be called a profession, given its lack of intellectual authority and underpinning. The huge growth in the demand for education was generated by the creation and expansion of business schools and the accompanying global rise in business influence and job creation. One could argue that the research in these subject areas was tagged along more as a result of the need for intellectual legitimation for teachers in the Universities, then from a puritan desire to develop sound and scientific accounting or finance theories and practices. Very crudely, it can be a passport to getting and keeping a well-paid job. If so, we should not then be surprised that a large majority of academics and researchers in these areas lack a genuine concern for the planet and its sustainability (Hopwood 2008) – they are merely doing a job which earns a decent salary, and research is done to keep the job and gain promotion or make money.

Mackenzie (2006) shows that finance research became 'an engine, not a camera', influencing financial innovation and practice, not always for sound ethical goals. It grew in status, power and influence, ultimately fuelling global booms and crashes. Recent experience has shown that what Warren Buffet calls 'weapons of mass destruction' (derivatives) were first conceived in the finance laboratory at the University or by finance academics who started their own hedge funds. Thus in finance, the values and conscience of the researcher are even more important, as they have a major influence on the design and construction of entire financial risk products, measurements and markets, which can have a big impact on the global financial system (Arnold 2009). We have already had plenty of human, social and environmental experience of the hugely adverse consequences of this science. Somehow, the sense of responsibility and public accountability is lacking. There is little humility to accompany such intellectual power.

In the early 1960s, Prof. David Solomons, one of the earliest professors of accounting in the world at the London School of Economics, wrote two articles very critical of professional training in accounting, insisting that future accountants must first get a University degree (Zeff 1995). The idea behind this was that professional practice requires sound theoretical and analytical training which can only be provided at a University. This was initially met with much criticism from the profession, but after the 1980s, it became more and more acceptable, and today is common practice in many parts of the world, though one can still get a professional accounting quali-fication without a University degree. In contrast to accounting, practice in finance does not require any formal professional training, and high finance was the preserve of mathematicians and rocket scientists in the early years, though now more formal training, like the Certified Financial Analyst qualification, have grown in importance and stature. In banking, there is a UK-based Institute of Bankers which provided professional training and certification, but its importance has waned of late, alongside the growth in scandals and frauds. Certainly, its membership is not a requirement for a job in finance today.

Ethics and behavioural training in both accounting and finance are rela-tively new phenomena, and virtually absent inside the University where technical approaches predominate. In business schools across North Amer-ica, there has been a growing requirement for ethics training, but often this is done as a standalone course on the side rather than integrated into indi-vidual subject disciplines like accounting or finance. Professional examina-tions in accounting are increasingly requiring some knowledge of ethics, but the teaching of this is abstract and philosophical, or primarily rule-based and therefore technical rather than personal and reflexive. In such circum-stances, students memorise what they need to know to pass the exam, rather than the education actually making a difference to their lives, character and conduct. One could argue that the University class/seminar format is not ideal for ethics training, which requires much more grassroots action, engagement, cultural analysis, discussion and reflection.

Parallel to these trends is the growth of stock markets, big business and globalisation and the multi-national corporation. Again as compared to human history on this planet, it is easy to forget that these developments have come from nowhere and in a very short time, have become a major force in human society. Scientists have recently coined the term 'Anthro-pocene' (Wikipedia), to highlight a period when human action is having an irreversible and adverse impact on the planet and its ecosystem, and it started sometime after the 1950s. The role of big business and selfish eco-nomics is critical to this destructive scenario, and accounting and finance, as components of this ideology, have had a devastating impact in enhancing human arrogance, hubris and dominion. These sciences are the 'weapons' through which economics perpetuated its neo-liberal materialistic ideology. A subject and science which was supposed to be a servant to society has now become its master and is dictating the terms of trade and human action (Shaxson and Christensen 2013; Kay 2015).

Whereas in the olden days most accountants and bankers would be serving owner-managed businesses, today they are advising anonymous managers of anonymous shareholders, where duty and responsibility are replaced by transactionalism and the 'me first' mentality. Not only has the research become abstracted from reality, even the practice of business and finance has become abstracted in the financialised Anthropocene, where no one cares about the medium or long term (Erturk et al., 2007 and 2008). A common phrase talked about in business and banking circles is 'I'll be gone, You'll be gone', something totally antithetical to sustainability. The neo-liberal era reduced the importance of common virtues and morality, making it easier for people not to fear dishonour or shame, as they did not belong to any faith or community. There is little personal self-regulation of conduct and behaviour, so many people try their utmost to discover ways of bending or breaking the rules to suit their pockets. If the professional certificate and qualification can help them to raise their status and profile, they will use it, but not give anything back to it if motivated by selfishness and greed. Loyalty to professional virtues and an ethical community is fast disappearing in modern society. How can there be any ethics when there is little fear or shame?

To be a teacher and scholar today who is critical of mainstream business in accounting and finance requires significant skill, courage and perseverance (Lehman 2013; McKernan 2011). Often the research funding for such work is not available, and there are limits to how much of it can be taught from accreditation constraints. So the research has to be conducted through one's own resourcefulness, and I suspect it is very difficult to sustain in countries where there is little support for research or no culture of critical enquiry exists. Good research requires years of training and dedication, and whilst academic journals set standards, they cannot provide training. In the last two decades, the power and influence of academic journals have increased significantly, creating a global race to publish, making it harder for people to retain research jobs and the freedom of enquiry needed to critique the business mainstream. One recent study showed that 95% of all articles published in top business journals today are pro-business (Harney and Dunne 2013). The power and reach of modern business have infiltrated the content of both teaching and research. The silencing has become subtle and very effective. That is why it is no surprise that businesses have continued to perpetuate massive frauds locally and globally (Cassidy 2002; Hightower 2004; Klein 2007; Moore 2001), with little academic challenge. As a society, we cannot afford to have an academy which becomes a servant of big business and its greed (Rajan and Zingales 2003). If so, we are a willing party to planetary and social destruction.

The aim of this book is to be constructive and to show the aspiring teacher or researcher ways in which accounting and finance education could become a force for good in society. In order to do that, we will go back to the basics of accounting and finance and restore the fundamentals which have either been forgotten or are being ignored and bypassed, consciously or subconsciously. We will make teaching personal and experiential, encouraging students to share their own knowledge and experience of finance, and the values and cultures which they bring to the classroom. This should help enable a much deeper and wider engagement with the subject, than the impersonal way in which it is being researched and taught today. We will then explore different methods of teaching which could help create this kind of revolution in the teaching and ethical engagement with accounting and finance knowledge and research. Finally, we will chart the new opportunities and possibilities that await us when such a radical approach is adapted to the teaching and research in this area.

If we were to do a survey of people's experiences with accountants or bankers or financial advisers, the kinds of emotions, phrases and adjectives we would hear are as follows:

> Fear, satisfaction, complexity, trust, deception, pain, confusion, anxiety, joy, tax problems, comfortable, luxury, sorrow, depression, worry, insecurity, unemployment, homelessness, relationship or marriage problems, over-indebtedness, loss of control, safety, expensive, greedy, selfish, lack of trust, cold and calculating, scary, distant, bankruptcy.

We should, therefore, ask how much of this is reflected in our teaching and research, and if not why not? If we disconnect our teaching from lived experience, what are we doing to the subject and the advancement of the discipline?

We could go on to wonder whether this disconnection with real-world experience has actually made us scholars and teachers also emotionless, cold and calculating. Has the content of our discipline forced us to become selfish and individualistic? To what extent is the technical complexity de-sensitising us from our students and their own beliefs and values? Is there truly a war between science and experience, where science is being forced to win and deny our emotional and subjective realities? Are we truly comfortable with our selfishness and egotism? Have we created a compartment in our minds between research and teaching, between making a living and caring for students? If so are we comfortable with this hypocrisy? Has our lack of religious belief been replaced by faith in our theories and objectivity, irrespective of the evidence? These are all critical questions that will be raised throughout this book.

Furthermore, the reality of modern-day inequality, and very high and rising costs of living, increases the need for quality jobs, and professional training is seen as a panacea for this. Lives have today become highly mortgaged, and we have now become slaves to finance, where a good job is the only means of survival. Finance has imposed a 'willing slavery' where the master and chains are not visible, and we are lied to about our freedom and independence. As a result, many people are forced to compromise their values and beliefs for the protection of the family. Graduate students face an increasingly high cost of housing and are virtually unable to buy their first property unless they get a high-paying starting job. Such jobs are only available for large greedy organisations who have mastered profit maximisation, and therefore graduates have to set their values aside for the sake of salary and status. The jobs marketplace eschews ethics silently and deliberately, just as the corporatisation of education does.

Scientists often have a strong desire to be 'morally neutral' and in the neo-liberal era, to allow the readers to make their own assumptions about what is right and wrong. However, there is no such thing as moral neutrality in practice. All knowledge and education are influenced by power and culture. There have been strong moves in recent decades towards positive research as opposed to normative research, whose aim is to try to explain the world in an unbiased way, using objective research methods and techniques. However, there has also been a growing resistance and a call for ethical research which is not afraid to take a moral position and to pursue lines of enquiry which try to deal with and resolve pressing human crises and challenges – something that would be called normative. It is argued throughout this book that the present global situation forces educators to take a moral position, and sitting on the fence is no longer affordable or right. It also requires educators to engage with the world, and not be afraid of speaking truth to power, and help prevent frauds and remove inequalities.

It is therefore assumed that the reader of this book is concerned about the state of modern accounting and finance, its cultural illiteracy and denial, its contribution to rising global inequality, corporate frauds and tax avoidance, and wants to do something about it. The attitude to teaching and research needs to be much beyond that of a job or vocation, and incorporate virtues such as caring, empathy, responsibility and accountability. There needs to be recognition that teachers are also role models for future professionals and need to walk their talk. The reader needs to be genuinely reflective about the teaching curriculum either within the University or in professional training and wants to nurture a future generation of graduates who are concerned about fairness, equality, sustainability and integrity. In the act of teaching, the reader wishes to engage students and help them to think for themselves, developing critical skills to help them evaluate business performance and valuation which does not compromise social and environmental responsibilities. Students are seen not as units in a factory production line, but individual souls and beings, willing to learn and develop their thinking, knowledge and experience. Above all, greed and selfishness are not invited into the classroom of the future, whose goal is to help nurture communities of caring and sharing, where responsibility is taken and not shirked.

If business education is to be effective, it must engage with the personal and the experiential. It can then build on this and in the process, help students make a much deeper connection with the subject matter they are studying and its meaning and purpose. In the process, they may get ignited from within and empowered to practice their knowledge in ways which could help build a more equal and inclusive society, at peace with the environment and society. The classroom could become a community of shared experience and learning, where students come with excitement and are able to bring their passion into the debates and forums. They may want to genuinely interact as they discover their own personal growth through the learning, not just something that needs to be done to pass an exam or get a grade or certificate. As educators in accounting and finance, we should count ourselves very lucky that we have such a huge audience wishing to learn and get certified, helping sustain our research and jobs.

One day, I decided to take my students on a field trip to the local Citizens Advice Bureau. This is a charity which helps people resolve personal problems relating to bills, benefits, taxes, debt, legal matters – through the provision of unbiased and expert advice, free of charge. I wanted my students to come to understand the everyday financial problems people face, and the variety of knowledge and skills required to help resolve them, including listening and counselling skills. The visit was quite a revelation about how difficult people find making everyday decisions about spending, borrowing, saving and surviving, and how scared they are to deal with financial matters. It helped them to have some idea of what an ethical accountant or finance person could do and how they can, if they wish, make a difference to their community and society. The feedback we got from the trip was very positive, and the students continue to talk about it and cite it in their essays. Some students ended up volunteering as advisers there.

Experiences like these help students to see the live and real nature of accounting and finance, and how good knowledge and its application can make a difference to ordinary lives. Isn't this what professionalism is really about – to serve the public objectively and independently, with a sense of care and compassion? Experience can be a great teacher of ethics and morality, without needing endless debates about what honesty means, or whether or not tax avoidance is legal. Doctors meet real people all the time and can see the results of their advice and prescriptions in the changing health of their patients. Many are empowered by this sense of service and often volunteer to provide free medical advice and care all over the world. Whilst we have international charities like Medicins Sans Frontiers, we do not have similar accounting or finance charities where professionals open regular clinics and give free advice and support.

A core assumption underlying this book is the natural law of interdependence. No man or woman is an island – we are all shaped by our histories, families, beliefs, experiences and communities. The whole planet is assumed to be an interdependent entity, where all living beings share its space and influence one another in various ways. To argue that man is the most important of these, or even the only one worthy of consideration by business, is deeply arrogant and misleading. The principles and ideas in this book recognise the interdependence of all life, and if anything, encourage the human being to become a caretaker and trustee of nature, rather than a master and owner. When we look at the etymology of the word individual, we find that it is that person who is indivisible – someone who cannot stand on their own. So in this book, we recognise the collective peoples and systems which help us become who we are, including nature, animals, the environment, faiths, diverse languages, different histories and nations and institutions. Just because animals or plants do not speak a language we understand does not mean that we ignore their stake and importance on the planet.

The intention of this book is to build a community of students and scholars who are concerned about the content and process of education, and willing to challenge and transform it. This outlook requires recognition of a shared existence and the urgency of making shared innovations and advances in education. We also assume that the reader is concerned about helping to create a better world, has a strong public conscience and is reflective about his or her teaching and research and its impact on society. Their life and exposure are such that readers are willing to discuss and listen to people from all walks of life, expert and otherwise, and open to learning from their experiences and curiosity. It is also assumed that the huge power and influence of accounting and finance on modern economy and society is understood, and the reader has a certain humility which comes from actively wanting to prevent hubris and arrogance.

In accounting, the professions have lately increased their emphasis on ethics training and education (Tweedie et al. 2013), without really understanding what it means. Ethics is also marginal to the main teachings, and often tagged as an add-on, rather than something which engages profoundly with the substance of professional training. Usually, ethical analysis stops at observing the law, or with loose concepts like independence, integrity and professional judgement, without engaging with personal culture and values and what makes the professional different from the trader or entrepreneur. More fundamentally, ethics are seen as a set of rules to be conformed to, rather than an opportunity for seeking meaning and purpose in professional work. Virtues like service, conscience and moral integrity are not explored beyond the superficial. As a result, the outcome is that students memorise the rules and answers without needing to change their conduct or character. Dilemmas, controversies and dialogue are avoided. Loeb (2015) suggests an active learning approach to teaching accounting ethics. There is also a lack of cultural diversity in the ethical theories that are discussed (Tweedie et al. 2013) and a thematic approach to teaching ethics has been suggested by them to encourage plural conversations.

There is growing evidence which shows that modern accounting and finance have more to do with politics and power, then to reason, fairness and market efficiency (Arnold 2009; Lehman 2013). For example, we now have a few very large international banks and accounting firms dominating the global landscape of accounting and finance. Their very size and influence are highly contradictory to the science of economics. Sadly, however, very rarely in the teaching curriculum of these subjects is the issue of politics introduced or debated. When I ask my students about their experience with their banks, most say that they are powerless, and the banks do not care for them when they need help and support. They feel disempowered, but somehow that experience is not normally allowed or acknowledged in classroom discussions. Neither is this impersonality reflected in contemporary banking textbooks, which highlight scientific practices of risk management, asset pricing and investment evaluation. In contrast, accounting educators have made a significant contribution to the research on sustainability and accountability, which is welcome and timely (see, e.g., Unerman et al. 2007; Gray and Bebbington 2001). This book examines the implications of these insights for reforming educational methods.

In summary, this opening chapter sets the scene for a major overhaul in the methods, content, culture and philosophy underlying accounting and finance education given the reality of social and environmental devastation. In this sense, it is provoking a revolution. The primary motive for this is the striking global evidence of corporate fraud, hubris, aggression, exploitation and hypocrisy where the logic and very construction of business enterprise is being questioned. Profound questions about the core assumptions and theories underlying economics, finance and accounting have been incorporated to open a new horizon of possibility for education which is moral, constructive, peace-making and environmentally sustainable. Different cultures and societies which inhabit the planet must not be forced to adopt a common theory of accounting and finance devoid of cultural and ethical sensibilities.

Instead, they should be encouraged to research, write and construct their own visions of an ethical and sustainable accounting and finance profession.

The next chapter goes back to the basics of accounting and finance. It probes the fundamental questions about accounting and finance, their inter-relationship which has been broken, and how we can reconstruct the subjects to make them more personal, ethical and sustainable. It does not provide new theories but makes a case for transforming the curriculum to make it more ethical and help build a virtuous society. It brings together a variety of research sources to show how this can be done, and explain why the change is both urgent and necessary. It calls for a substantial transformation of the content and methods of accounting and finance education. It argues that such a transformation will make both teaching and learning more fun, engaging, creative and sustainable.

2 Back to basics

There seems to be a war between finance and ethics. The 'success' of finance erodes ethics, and the success of ethics would reduce the power, influence and status of finance. The more money permeates society, the more it erodes culture. As explained earlier, Graeber (2014) is an anthropologist by profession, and when he investigated the history of finance, he discovered that for thousands of years, finance was only about culture, faith, politics and relationships. It was not technical and complex, nor a subject to be taught or researched, but a practice to be lived and shared. Social relationships and exchange were critical to society, and often money was not allowed to dominate relationships. Taxation played a key role in the history of money creation and state finance, and wealth was an instrument of power and control. Rarely did money play an overwhelming role in society or one which completely overpowered it. It had a role to play, but other factors also influenced power, trade, regulation and governance. It is, therefore, critical that students are exposed to the fundamentals of accounting and finance and its history and politics.

Accounting is not just about big companies and their financial statements. Similarly, finance is not just about investments, discounting, valuation, complex derivatives and risk. For students to really understand these disciplines, they must first understand the basics and be taught how the present is connected to the past. People, even students, encounter accounting and finance on a daily basis, but perhaps do not see it as that. Trust, honesty and confidence are very important, but not easily measurable or valued and placed on a balance sheet. Ignoring their valuation gives the impression as if they do not matter.

A bill at a supermarket is a type of account. A student loan or a bank overdraft is a type of finance. However, if you read contemporary textbooks in these subjects, they are very far from these basics and technically complex with their own jargon and arithmetic. Subconsciously, the complexity suggests the need for advanced training whilst at the same time hiding or even deliberately confusing the fundamental values that underlie the teaching. For example, derivatives are often presented as hedging or risk management tools, when in reality, they are used for gambling and speculation, and have become completely disconnected from fundamentals. Weak foundations make for bad science. In this chapter, we will explore the fundamentals of accounting and finance, and see whether what is being taught in their name today is fact, science or fiction.

The 2008 global financial crisis cost hundreds of billions of dollars, leading to large government bailouts and forced mergers and consolidations of big banks. Many of the large institutions at the centre of the crisis later grew in size and influence, and created new frauds to sustain their greed even after they were rescued. Some (Engelen et al. 2012; Kay 2011; Kay 2015; Das 2011; McSweeney 2009; Shah 2017; Gendron and Smith-Lacroix 2013) have argued that the blame for the crash should go as much to the mistaken ideology of finance, disguised as science, which led to substantial deregulation and excessive hubris, without care or concern for the consequences or risk for society. Surprisingly, even the core discipline and teachings of finance have failed to change after the crisis, and the textbooks have gone global, standardising and spreading the strong original biases of profit maximisation and greed as the only way to succeed in business (see e.g. Ross et al. 2012; Deegan and Ward 2013). Often these assumptions are hidden or undeclared, and very rarely are students allowed to engage in discussion about their truthfulness and modern-day accuracy. As accounting has come to play a subsidiary role to finance, it has continued to promote the 'religion' of shareholder primacy and wealth maximisation, with little reflection on the fundamental crash of ideology that was revealed in the 2008 crisis. Formulaic standardised teaching has continued to meet the demands of the business education factory, and cash reserves have grown in spite of the crash. The competition for jobs has been very profitable for the selling of business education – upgrading skills and qualifications may increase a student's chances of getting a better job, as the promise goes. The real-world impact on student jobs, productivity, career success and business growth is rarely evaluated or measured.

There are growing gaps between theory and practice, both in finance and in accounting, which are very concerning. In addition, professional practice has become highly institutionalised, with the result that members learn a variety of skills at work rather than through formal education and training. These workplaces are often large and global, where norms and behaviours are increasingly commercial. Primary ethics and values like integrity and independence, and the openness to question and critique, get challenged and compromised in such environments. Conformity often becomes the norm, and politics replaces culture and personal ethics. Raw commercial power is able to buy or fire any skill set at short notice. People inside such organisations can be increasingly insecure and therefore silenced. Even whistleblowing is suppressed and punished (Heffernan 2011) when the opposite needs to prevail in an open and sustainable society.

One major arena where the cracks in accounting and finance education have been opened widely is around taxation and offshore secrecy (Tax Justice Network 2015; Picciotto 2007; Palan et al. 2010; Shaxson 2012). In finance, tax is taught as a cost to business, and, therefore, minimising that cost is the right way to maximise profits. There is no discussion about how to minimise it or what is legitimate ethically and what is not. In fact, more generally, one very popular global finance textbook claims very early on that to the extent that companies focus on maximising shareholder value, we consider all their actions to be ethical (Ross et al. 2012). Some scholars have become so disillusioned by corporate conduct and spin that they have even announced 'the end of corporate social responsibility' (Fleming and Jones 2012). Although tax raises very profound questions about the ethics of accounting and finance, these questions are largely avoided in business schools and have had no impact on the content of the teaching of accounting and finance.

Whilst openness and transparency are increasingly promoted in accounting and finance textbooks and theories, corporations are trying their darndest to be secretive, opaque and outright fraudulent in their reporting and communications (McBarnet and Whelan 1999). Recent scandals dubbed as LuxLeaks and Panama Papers expose the involvement of some of the world's largest corporations. Corporations, accounting firms and billionaires routinely use accounting, law and finance to hide the true motives behind their transactions, to minimise tax and to avoid transparency of large chunks of profits from different countries and jurisdictions. Far from increasing accountability, the evidence shows that many large and powerful organisations are fully capable of managing and manipulating their transactions and information flows to subvert any kind of regulation or governance (Shaxson 2012). A simple example of this is country-by-country reporting for multi-national corporations, something which is being strongly resisted, but completely contradicts the logic of informational usefulness for shareholders (Palan et al. 2010). At present, the accounts of global companies do not break down profits and performance by each country where they do business. This makes a mockery of the accountability of corporate financial statements.

Some have argued and scientifically demonstrated that we live in an era of 'financialisation' (Zwan 2014; Froud et al. 2006), where there has been a growing dominance of finance over and above the real productive economy. What was seen as a means to do business has now become an end in itself, with dire consequences for wider society. Research has demonstrated that the size of the finance sector relative to the real economy has grown significantly in the last four decades. Educators are teaching students how to make money from money, with the least effort and the highest reward. There is a disconnect between effort and reward leading to what some call a 'rentier' economy, where the financier is an extractor of wealth from the economy rather than a contributor to growth and development (Sayer 2016). If this process encourages greed, vice and corruption, as we have witnessed in large blue chip corporations like Enron, WorldCom, Shell, Rolls Royce, Goldman Sachs, Lehman Brothers, Volkswagen, presumably none of that is the responsibility of the educators – they are objective scientists focused on testing theories! Somehow, finance and economics have succeeded in disguising their fundamental values and assumptions, and built a big house of cards above them, which keeps defrauding and failing society. Yet the discipline survives intact. It has managed to cushion its responsibility and accountability to society, and deny its fundamental moral conflicts and fraudulent ideologies.

Financialisation has meant that scholars, professional firms and experts in accounting and finance have often risen to positions of significant power and influence, possibly even leading to hubris given the egoism of intellectuals. This has resulted from the growing demand for their expertise and the increasing need for education and training created by the plentiful jobs. Unlike many disciplines, it is never difficult for Universities to recruit students in accounting or finance. They just come without much convincing or effort and are willing to pay the fees due to the likelihood of a well-paid job at graduation. We know from human history that power often leads to hubris and corruption. It is therefore imperative that we become aware of this power and develop a deep humility and sensitivity to the peoples, institutions and societies adversely affected by it. In my opinion, the lack of reform in accounting and finance education in spite of the global financial crises suggests a deeper arrogance and lack of concern and accountability. Such a situation is unsustainable if our intention is that knowledge and education are dedicated to building a peaceful, harmonious and sustainable society where business acts transparently, responsibly and ethically.

The ideas in this book deliberately put business in its wider context and assume a common desire for creating a peaceful, harmonious and sustainable planet. Human respect for one another, including the variety of cultural histories and religious beliefs that inhabit our planet, is also central to the vision expressed. Diversity is seen as a natural law of the universe, and instead of denying or suppressing it, it needs to be acknowledged and respected in the teaching of business. Our different cultures are also different theories of living and working on this planet and must not be ignored just because they are not taught in an elite business school. History and fundamentals should not be suppressed or ignored, nor should we assume that modernity is by definition better than tradition, or current society better than previous societies. Similarly, when we use arithmetic and calculation, we must be fully aware of both its strengths and its limitations. In an increasingly globalised world, we are much more aware of one another's similarities and differences, and to deny this in the classroom is to create and perpetuate a fiction. Somehow, both accounting and finance education have a way of suppressing human culture and society. This is unsustainable.

In some of my classes, I get experts from industry to address the students. For example, when I ask the local general manager of Handelsbanken, Mr Andrew Pike, to lecture my students about the process of loan evaluation, I find that a lot of what he is saying is not reflected in the finance textbooks. He places a lot of emphasis on character and conduct, and on references and relationships in evaluating loan applications. In the finance textbook, there is no theory of the lending or borrowing 'process' – instead, it is assumed that if the right business proposal is presented, loans will be approved independent of any personality or relationship. Process seems irrelevant to the science of finance, even though for ordinary people, process is as important as outcome.

More generally, I notice a lack of respect for experience as a professional. This Handelsbanken manager had 30 years of experience in banking and drew from it in his loan evaluations. What this suggests is that a formulaic approach to business education cannot understand or appreciate experience as a virtue, as this could potentially decry the need for academic training. Education methods and processes have distanced themselves from the real world, instead of engaging with business practice – this devalues practical experience and diminishes its relevance and tacit knowledge. In medicine, professors are also clinicians, seeing patients alongside their teaching and research, keeping them connected and grounded. This is rare in business education today, in spite of the fact that business is such a practical discipline. Raw experience and wisdom can also be gained if professors go into communities and listen to their questions and experiences of how business influences their lives and mental health and well-being.

The idea of a teaching or learning factory is relatively new and becomes deeply problematic at higher levels of education, where students need to learn to think and critique ideas and concepts by themselves. To see teaching and education as a business transaction, where a University gives a brand name but does not really care much about the student engagement or experience is a relatively modern invention. Similarly, a wealthy professor was often seen as a contradiction to the profession of teaching and learning. More fundamentally, money, wealth and materialism were at times seen with disdain, and definitely not the be all and end all of life. What was valued more were relationships, equality and community, and in many cultures, animals and nature were seen as playing a strong part of the wider society (see e.g. Ekins et al. 1992; Shah and Rankin 2017).

The present-day teaching of accounting and finance is highly abstract and impersonal. Instead of engaging with students' practical experiences of managing and handling finance, the subject and teaching methods try to be distant and abstract. There is no remorse or shame in doing this. In the real world, students need to budget to manage their income and expenses, and they often come from families where finance has been a problem or a challenging experience. In planning for their future jobs and lifestyles, they will need to understand mortgages, savings and investments. I find that many already have negative marks on their personal credit files and feel overpowered by the reality of financial monitoring and control. In my opinion, it is therefore much more effective to talk about such matters first in personal terms, so that they can engage with the subject matter and not see it as too distant or corporate. The subjective experiences enhance the overall learning experience. A formulaic approach where there are large class sizes would not be suitable to such engagement, so perhaps that is why it is avoided altogether. Holistic education means engaging with the whole person, including his/her lived experiences and existing knowledge and wisdoms. The first year foundation of accounting and finance training should have a personal base, helping students to relate the discipline to the real world and remove its jargon and complexity.

The abstraction from personal lives and experiences is deeply unhealthy for several reasons. Firstly, it subconsciously gives the impression that the students' personal lives and experiences are worthless and irrelevant. The experience of learning becomes one of super-imposed facts and techniques, shaping future professionals who may continue the process of depersonalisation by using jargon and abstract techniques and formulae to confuse their clients and exploit their ignorance. This is profoundly wrong and unethical. It also removes the scope for diverse cultural knowledges and experiences from entering the classroom, thereby suppressing cultural difference and identity. Such methods give students the impression that their own views and cultural differences do not matter when it comes to accounting and finance, when in reality, they do matter significantly. If empathy is not practiced and demonstrated through example in the classroom, how are future professionals going to learn and practice it in the workplace?

There seems to be a fundamental conflict between people and systems in business education. A systems approach leads to analyses of methods, techniques and processes, whereas a humane approach leads to ethics, culture, psychology and social and environmental impact. One approach pretends to be ethically neutral and objective, and the other does not deny human subjectivity and social and environmental complexity. By definition, the systems approach is often technocratic and idealistic, pretending there is no politics or inequality. In life, we see both people and systems, and neither can live without the other. Systems are also very rarely permanent but instead always contingent and changed by people and politics (Said 1993). Accounting and finance both operate as parts in systems of operation of businesses and influence the methods of conduct as well as measurement and interpretation. As already explained, there is a fascinating range of interdisciplinary research in accounting which tries to integrate people and systems and exposes the benefits and conflicts of the two. Sadly, this is virtually absent in finance. As lecturers and professors, we would need to question why this is so. Ethics and culture are profound ways in which the analysis of people and systems can be integrated.

History is the story of the larger human experience, over generations, societies and hundreds of years of time. It helps us understand why we are where we are today and learn about past successes and failures with the hope that we do not repeat the same mistakes. History does not happen in boxes or disciplinary boundaries, and its trajectory may not always be neat or even predictable. Booms and crashes in finance have become normalised, but if their history and experience are not taught in the classroom, students may end up thinking that the present times are the best and most modern and civilised.

This lack of historical memory could breed arrogance and hubris, making some leaders feel that the rewards are entirely due to their personal skill and efforts. If instead learners studied accounting and financial history (see e.g. Edwards and Walker 2009), they would discover the significant roles played by fraud, politics and power, and even large businesses and market abuses, which devastated societies. They may find that accounting's role and importance has changed over time and that there was a time when there were debtor prisons for those who could not pay their loans back. History would help them understand how the structures of societies, markets and institutions affected the practice of accounting and finance in profound ways. To not teach history is to deny students from learning the truth. That is surely wrong for any University.

In fact, there is a fundamental war between science and history which is accentuated by the disciplinary organisation of knowledge that we have today. Experts would rather have their science become complex and sophisticated then to necessarily relate to human experience and history; otherwise, what is unique about their knowledge as compared to the wisdom of ordinary people or social groups and even historians? Daly and Cobb (1994) analyse this problem rigorously and consider it particularly acute in the field of economics, which is the parent of both accounting and finance. Even moral philosophers like Adam Smith and Alfred Marshall had a strong sense of history and did not wish their writings to be abstracted from the real world or from social and public accountability. So it seems the ignorance of history and human experience in many parts of accounting and finance teaching is not accidental but deliberate. University structures, disciplinary organisation and recruitment criteria and incentives may accentuate this behaviour. Experts want to worship their disciplines and practice disciplonatory to protect their jobs, rewards and status. In transforming accounting and finance education, the challenge is, therefore, very significant, as the expert police and guardians are deeply entrenched.

The ignorance of culture and social psychology perpetuates the distancing of business from sensitivity to society and the environment, and makes profit and greed an automaton whose science and purpose is beyond question. Impersonal education can easily justify cold calculating behaviour, something which is far from the true nature of any human being. Coldness leads to insecurity, isolation and loneliness. It leads to fear and mistrust. It builds walls instead of bridges. This deliberate ignorance is a fraud at the very heart of business education. The deceit is even more concerning given the importance of accounting and finance, and the vast influence it holds on the business world.

When education is deliberately made impersonal, it may satisfy the need for objectivity but at the same time destroy the potential to humanise and engage students. Many MBA programmes require students to have business experience prior to enrolment. I find that taking students on field trips to local businesses, banks or accounting firms helps them to really understand the wider context of the subject and its practical challenges and possibilities. Students get really motivated to learn, and even films and broadcasts help them to really connect with business news and events. It enhances their learning of business jargon. It is worth making the effort and the sacrifice to give lasting experiences and memories for students who are at the beginning of their professional careers.

In fact, when academics focus their energies on writing and publishing research papers, they are indirectly being very selective about their theories and data. Even though business conduct may be multi-disciplinary, business schools are still divided in subject and disciplinary boundaries, where often the faculty do not engage across disciplines even though they are working in the common field of business enterprise. Competition and journal rankings have forced them to narrow their focus, separating the disciplines even more. Most business academics outside of finance would not today be able to understand a single journal article published in eminent journals like *Journal of Finance* or *Journal of Financial Economics*, so caged they are in technical jargon and complex mathematical and statistical analysis. These journals are unashamed to protect their territories in spite of this opacity from critique. They have become a power unto themselves. One could even argue that just as the banks have consolidated their hold after the 2008 crash, so have the finance journals and their underlying theories and ideologies. If anything, their power and hold on the discipline has increased after the crash and globalised even more. If academics earn their 'bonuses' from publication in top journals, then, in the same way that we criticise bankers' bonuses, we must question the problems of perverse incentives in the pursuit of true knowledge and wisdom.

According to Said (1993), specialisation leads to laziness, myopia and a silencing of creativity and dialogue. The specialist intellectuals become closed-minded, and instead of opening and sharing their knowledge, they belong to an increasingly small cabal of like-minded people steeped in their own jargon and mutual appreciation. They take pride in the closure of the discipline and its 'scientific' sophistication, where *they* have defined both the science and the complexity. Intellectuals also become deeply insecure in the process and see external challenge as a threat to their expertise. In both accounting and finance, one of the most serious outcomes of this specialisation is a complete closure of discussions around ethics and leadership in the textbooks. Both leadership and ethics are huge topics for business schools, often taught as whole modules, but in accounting and finance, they are largely avoided.

In fact, specialisation leads to control of knowledge whereby the only people who can teach are the experts, and the role of students becomes one of passive listening and absorption. The act of research and teaching can become one where power is concentrated and others are destroyed, marginalised or disempowered. This seems completely antithetical to the whole openness of scientific enquiry. Such practices go against the grain of holistic education, and it is therefore no surprise that imagination and resistance dissipate in this environment. For learners, the whole experience of this can be very disempowering. The present dean of Harvard Business School, Prof. Nitin Nohria started his career as a PhD student in finance at MIT, but very quickly moved to studying leadership instead and rose to become a world expert (Source: Wikipedia). He must have found finance narrow and limiting, and leadership more creative and reflective. The subsequent record of his success shows he took the right decision.

The rewards of modern business education seem to be warped against good teaching and student inspiration and transformation. Furthermore, theory can also distance academics from the messiness of the real world, where incidents and situations do not happen in tiny disciplinary boxes but often through interactions of a wide range of disciplines and factors. In fact, the exponential growth of the Big 4 accounting firms in recent decades has come precisely from their interdisciplinary skills and ability to understand a wide range of business problems, something which the academy seems increasingly incapacitated to do. Disciplonatory, where academics feel cosy in disciplinary or theoretical boundaries, something especially true in modern finance, can lead to a worship of science and close the window of genuine critique and curiosity.

A lot of advanced research and training in both accounting and finance tends to happen within large financial institutions like the Big 4 global accounting firms – Deloitte, PWC, EY and KPMG, or global banks like Goldman Sachs, J P Morgan Chase, HSBC, Barclays, Citibank, etc. Given their size and resources, they are able to hire the most talented individuals, so they already have a head start in terms of skills and knowledge. Such internal training and mentoring may be formal or informal, and can be interdisciplinary, where teams of people from different backgrounds, like lawyers, accountants and management consultants, come together to advise on a merger or acquisition or an efficient corporate structure which maximises tax avoidance and corporate secrecy.

The knowledge and skills generated by such financial monoliths are internal to the firm (Nordenflycht 2010) and largely kept as a corporate secret. Their motives are private and profit oriented, making the research and knowledge partial and biased. Every now and again, these institutions publish thought pieces and research studies, but rarely are these done in cooperation with academics or public intellectuals. Often they are crafted in such a way as to be subtle marketing exercises, helping to sell their skills and services by increasing fear among clients and offering a helping hand, for a fee of course. Changes in regulation are great opportunities for profit for these firms (Shah 2015b). Unlike Universities, they are primarily profit maximising global institutions with enormous power and influence, but little by way of public interest or ethical conscience. There has been considerable evidence about how government funds have been expropriated by these firms either through helping corporates minimise their taxes (Brooks 2014; Palan et al. 2010) or through high-risk banking which has required multi-billion dollar state bailouts. It may also be that they possess advanced skills which could benefit accounting and finance education and innovation, but rarely do these come back into the classroom. It suits the firms very well if academics do not challenge their conduct and practices, and quietly do work which is irrelevant and self-competing. If academics were to challenge their knowledge and conduct, there could be trouble in terms of gaining professional legitimacy.

In a similar way, there is a dearth of research which looks at the impact of business education and the degree to which it actually helps businesses grow and succeed (Pettigrew and Starkey 2016). Many famous Universities in the world like Chicago or Columbia are not far from very poor and deprived areas. This exposes the bubble in which academics operate where they have little engagement with their own immediate neighbourhoods and their economic, employment and business problems. Instead, there is huge focus on the teaching production line, and volumes of research are being generated, but little impact assessment on what difference it actually makes in society. Questions like does it lead to better productivity or efficiency, or does it create more inequality and greed urgently need to be addressed, given the vast resources which go into business education. According to Pfeffer and Fong (2002), the outcomes of business education are often very modest or poor, and it does not generate the training and value that businesses often seek. Some have even argued that the primary blame for modern business frauds and practices lies at the heart of the education and training of students. The system teaches them to be greedy and selfish, so why are we surprised with the result. One of the chief executives of HBOS, Andy Hornby, which was the largest corporate failure in British history, was educated at Harvard Business School, where he was the top-performing student. Similarly, Skilling, one of the key architects of the Enron fraud, was also educated at Harvard.

It may be that some business students are already instrumental to begin with, so if we are facing a fundamental crisis in business behaviour and education, reform should happen outside the business school, in humanities departments like sociology or political science or even history. This is where radical understanding and analysis can be easily mobilised, and critiques and transformative leaders developed. In these classes, it may be easy to express the frauds and contradictions of business, and students do not expect to be pro-business or make big returns on their educational investments. Students in these subjects are more likely to understand the fundamental nature of social and environmental responsibility, and learn and develop the new tools and techniques required to bring sustainable and ethical innovations to fruition at a time when the world needs them so urgently (Pehlivanova and Martinoff 2015).

Students often come to education with specific needs, such as a job at graduation or a formula for a fast-growing business start-up. If they want to be materialistic and selfish, critical theories and truths may make them uncomfortable, and this may translate into student complaints or even rebellions. A teaching experiment about critical accounting conducted by Chabrak and Craig (2013) revealed that students engage very well with such ideas, but do get concerned when it comes to their careers and personal futures – they experience a kind of cognitive dissonance. In a time when student feedback and satisfaction is highly valued by most employers, and can also be made very instantly public through social media, it can be very tricky to present critical theories. These are never discussed in professional accounting training or discourse at all, making student experiences factual and technical rather than reflective and analytical.

As we have seen already, at the root, money is a human creation and has a relatively short history compared to human life on this planet. We must not make out as if it is objective and value-free, nor that its use is a fundamental good in society. It is important to understand the limits of money and its many subjectivities for us to practice accounting and finance in a sustainable way. It is also important to recognise the limits of measurement and accountability – not all that is good in life can be measured, nor is accounting and accountability perfect or good in all circumstances. For example, there were times in human history when there were strong communities of trust and mutuality, where a large part of life was conducted without any money or measurement. The levels of trust reduced the need for accounting and accountability. Such times led to equality, peace and harmony, something which we often lack today.

Trust and human capital are very important to the running of any business, but not measured or valued in the financial statements. In some sense, they are beyond measure, but not valuing them also implies that they are not important or critical to the business. The finance and accounting systems endorse the devaluation of these very important qualities and virtues of any organisations. This is a very political statement, yet the financial statements with their neat calculations and balance sheets make them disappear in an objective and scientific way. Students in class could be exposed to these flaws to enable them to understand the limits of finance and accounting.

There are many other types of capital which are very important in life besides financial capital. Examples of this include natural capital, relationship capital, physical capital, trust capital, community capital, gender capital, ethical capital, knowledge capital, emotional capital, health capital – all of these are very important but somehow excluded from both accounting and finance. We can discuss in class what these forms of capital mean and how valuable they are for a healthy society and planet. This can help students understand the wider context of capital and the limits of finance. Students may even progress to challenge how financial capital is destroying other more lasting and sustainable forms of capital through its greed, expropriation and selfishness.

Education and learning traditionally involved a strong component of human interaction and engagement. There was a relationship between the student and the teacher. In my own Jain culture, the thirst for knowledge and wisdom is highly respected and even regarded as sacred and divine. In many societies, teaching was seen as a very honourable profession, and instead of giving facts and formulae to students, the teacher acted as a catalyst to spark a profound inner quest for truth and meaning among his/ her students. In India, the 'guru'/teacher was seen as a person who enables the student to discover his/her own inner light and potential. As a result, the whole philosophy of education was very different. By respecting students as whole beings, we begin to engage their full personalities, not just their brains and analytical abilities. Payment of fees for learning was nominal at best in many societies, and teachers did not see knowledge as a product to be traded or exploited, but something that was sacred and needed to be shared rather than patented.

When a professor takes an ethical approach to education seriously, he/ she needs to be reflexive about his/her own motivations for teaching and research, and the social impact and sustainability of such behaviour. In a way, professors need to look at the mirror first and choose what they believe in and stand for. They would need to develop an active social and environmental conscience, and move from individualism to communitarian thinking and actions. Care would need to be applied to the research topics chosen and the methods adapted, and the ways in which students are respected and taught. Cultural and other forms of diversity such as gender, sexuality, disability all need to be respected. Professors need to understand the limits of intellectualism and expertise, and respect the world of practice where often people have to make judgements and compromises simply to survive. Ideally, there should be a concern to help those who are marginalised in society and help reduce the exploitation that happens through accounting and finance. In return, professors would find a sense of meaning and purpose in their work and a deep satisfaction from empowering students to become responsible and ethical citizens of society.

Languages were created by villages and communities to enable communication and shared understanding. In a similar way, we can look at accounting and finance as modern languages of business (Graham 2013) to help achieve certain goals and priorities. The more sophisticated a language, the more exclusive it becomes, and in the process, it can lead to power and authority. This language can prevent non-expert others from criticising it, as they do not understand the language which shaped the science and truth; it can ex-communicate many people and thereby exclude them from critique and challenge. Some argue that the modern language and institutions of accounting and finance are cursed (Shaxson and Christensen 2013; Mitchell and Sikka 2011), and far from spreading equality and cohesion, they are instead authorising fraud and exploitation, breaking and corrupting society in the process. Such claims need to be examined, as they could have a profound influence on the new kinds of training and education needed to build a sustainable planet.

Fundamentally, there is a real tension and conflict between technical and, therefore, rule-based and calculative education, and qualitative or analytical learning, which requires students to make judgements based on a range of criteria, not all of which may be measurable or calculable, but are important nonetheless. Technical training tends to emphasise method, rules, accuracy and calculation and de-emphasise abstractions, assumptions, judgement and limitations. The real world of business is often much more complex than just a calculation or application of technical rules. The accounting profession is increasingly emphasising the importance of inter-personal and social skills in the making of a successful professional, even though the examinations are primarily technical. There seems to be an inherent failure in recognising the conflict between the two modes of thinking. It takes special people to be able to balance the two skills, and leaders tend to be those who are very good at social and inter-personal skills, and delegate the technical work to others. Different methods of teaching and understanding these subjects can be complementary, but to avoid them entirely would be to mislead students about the truth of accounting and finance.

The very idea of profit is often seen as sacrosanct in business. It is a key measure of performance and beyond question. Even its maximisation is seen as an objective good, endorsed by economic science. However, many argue that this is far from the truth. Profit calculation involves very profound assumptions about what we choose to measure as revenues and costs, what we choose to exclude and often hides the subjectivity of such measurements. For example, all companies depend on the state for the provision of roads, energy, security, law and order, health, education, banking system, social cohesion and so on. These services cost money, and the tax system has been designed as a way for the government to collect the revenues to support these services. If governments cannot collect these revenues, they will not be able to provide the services which businesses depend upon. When tax is seen as a cost instead of a payback to government for these critical business services, profit calculation undermines the very fabric of a peaceful and fair society. Even worse, when accounting and finance professionals help corporations to minimise their taxes using their knowledge of the laws and regulations, they are participating in a profound betrayal of the social contract which gave rise to corporations in the first place.

I feel that in contemporary business education, profound discussions on ethics and morality are scary to many professional academics. They are perceived as subjective matters and, therefore, not relevant or necessary. A core reason for this is that if we look at the recent history of science, morality has been admonished in the interests of objectivity, and facts are more important than moral principles, as if all facts are free of ethical presumptions. Science has deliberately separated knowledge from experience, encouraging the impersonality of the student experience. Education has become highly institutionalised through large and wealthy Universities, whose business schools often depend on big donations and endowments from wealthy bene-factors or corporations. The links between pure un-conflicted knowledge and wisdom and truth have been broken. Replacing it is an increasing certi-fication of business knowledge and a separation of academic conduct from the morality and ethics of the scholar. The character of the *guru* is no longer important to his/her ability to teach, inspire and enlighten student develop-ment and growth.

According to most faith traditions, in essence, human beings are spiri-tual beings, not material or mechanistic bodies which live from external programming or regulations. According to Molisa (2011), this is the funda-mental problem with contemporary accounting and finance education as it completely denies the inner truth about every human being. In his research, he draws upon many faith traditions and the work of the contemporary mys-tic Eckhart Tolle, which has shaped many profound transformations. For Molisa, the identification with the body as opposed to the soul is where greed, aggression, vice, ego, bondage, desire and insecurity lies. To trans-form society and the environment, we must transform our inner selves and spirits first. Otherwise, we will not get very far and unwittingly perpetuate anger, selfishness and aggression as opposed to love and compassion. When education is spirit centred, it leads to a profound inner transformation from which emancipation or true freedom become spontaneous. When we are in tune with our inner consciousness, we become really enlightened and awakened, Molisa explains.

This is a deeply ethical approach to accounting and finance, and one which deserves to be taken very seriously. It has resonance and impact on all business education and practice, and challenges the core of the modern approach to teaching and education. Unless we awaken our students from within, we will make no lasting or sustained difference. Whilst the critique and discussions may lead to different information and exposure, the highly institutionalised workplaces will quickly make them fall into line with cor-porate rules and demands. If we are not careful, our theories and radical ideas will remain in the classroom, and academics will keep on talking to one another rather than having a wider impact on society.

In particular, the highly political nature of accounting, which has been so widely researched, is ignored in professional education and often in Univer-sity courses which are professionally accredited. This reveals how unrealis-tic and biased professional accounting courses have become. Students often focus on education brand names, the grades and results and building a job-ready CV. There are also very real economic pressures on them which can-not be denied. Quality jobs are becoming very rare and highly competitive, and the costs of living are rising all the time. What matters to many students is the grade of their courses rather than the content of the learning, let alone the truthfulness and honesty of the educational system and process. In an age of industrialisation and widespread competition, students are often forced to be very instrumental.

The most basic element of both accounting and finance is money. We create a 'fallacy of misplaced concreteness' if we turn money into something that is real and permanent (Daly and Cobb 1994). Its value changes over time and is not fixed, sometimes depreciating dramatically and without warning. Just as it is born, it can also die, and there are plenty of examples in history of the death of currencies. Because money is a unit of account, it makes accounting and finance simple to apply, as mathematics can now be applied to aspects such as debt calculation, interest rates, pricing and even risk measurement. However, in all these areas, the limits of money and calculation should not be forgotten, and the beauty and sophistication of mathematics should not be allowed to overwhelm the true values and assumptions which underlie the calculations. The 2008 crash was partly fuelled by misleading calculations and biases, and raw greed which encouraged people 'to keep dancing until the music stops', without listening to the music or understanding the economy (Ferguson 2012).

There are two key elements here in undergraduate training – one is the explanation of the fundamentals and related to the history and origins of accounting and finance. The other is the link between the fundamentals and the current theories and technologies of accounting and financial measurement and construction. When this is genuinely done, the result will not be comfortable for many modern academics, as they have been happily teaching a tower of babel without showing the cracks in the foundations over decades. Whole careers and reputations have been built on this. For new teachers of accounting and finance, such an approach is a tremendous opportunity to create something new and really excite students to question and challenge existing theory and practice.

Such an approach also opens the opportunity of cultural and ethical diversity in the teaching methods and content of accounting and finance education. It allows lecturers from different parts of the world to bring their own local perspectives on accounting and finance. Professors can introduce local ethics and business character, diversity of practices and allow students to bring their own experiences of accounting and finance into the classroom. In this way, there is likely to be much better engagement and dialogue, and a richer appreciation of the diverse nature of both accounting and finance.

As an example, let us look at 'traditional' markets, a concept celebrated and revered in modern finance, but something which has become hugely distorted from its origins. Students are likely to have had first-hand experience of these, as they do exist in some ways all over the world – whether it is the fruit and vegetable market or the tourist market or even a car-boot sale. In a traditional market, a trader goes not only to make profits and become rich but also to meet people, both customers and other traders, to haggle and sell and to make enough to feed the family, until the next day. Rarely do these people have an ambition to become millionaires. Often they are passionate about what they are selling, develop the skills of selling, speak many languages and know about relationships and dialogue. We can ask students to reflect on the roles of accounting and finance in these markets. We can ask them to think about risk, return, valuation, pricing, profit and even cash flow and wealth. For them to do so would not require sophisticated training in accounting and finance. Learners would be able to relate much better to the subject and use their experience to answer the questions.

Such an exercise can open up a range of discussions about the fundamentals of business, the different types and expectations of entrepreneurs, the social rôle of both money and trading and the joys of personal connection and community. When we then ask students to switch from this to the stock market and explore the similarities and differences, a whole new range of enquiries can open up. First and foremost is the absence of a people connection – there is no face to face meeting in stock trading, as most of it is done electronically. What is gained and what is lost when this happens? Is it possible that in the absence of contact, it becomes much easier to cheat and defraud? Case studies about recent market frauds could be introduced here to show how anonymity helps the trader to forget that he/she is being deceitful, or makes deceit a normalised behaviour.

How many finance academics or textbooks discuss the stock market in this way? If they do not, can we see how the abstract nature and content of teaching actually helps students to disconnect more and more from the real world? This is something which will prevent them from seeing the pain and suffering caused to people and the environment by their actions. Is this the outcome we seek through our education systems and methods? Do we really want to confuse our students with our advanced knowledge and retain power over them, or to ignore their future aspirations of building a safe, equal and inclusive world? Can we as scholars and academics endorse a system which has become fundamentally greedy and fraudulent, and instead of taking an ethical position, just do our jobs and teach what we have always taught? Such deeper reflections are the call of our time.

Question marks are being raised about the profound incompatibility of compound interest with nature and growth (Daly and Cobb 1994). Whilst money can grow exponentially, nature cannot and is limited by space and time. Positive interest rates create a profound economic inequality and unsustainability, which many faith traditions like Christianity and Islam criticised and questioned in the past (Daly and Cobb 1994; Kamla 2015). Given that money is a human creation, it seems that with the concept of unearned financial income (interest), we have let a genie out of the bottle which we have no way of controlling. There is absolutely no reflexivity about interest rates and discount rates in accounting and finance education whatsoever. In truth, interest rates play a significant role in creating global inequality and sustaining it (Coggan 2012; Graeber 2014).

Similarly, scholars are asking profound questions about 'rentiers' and financial extractors (Sayer 2016; Whyte and Wiegratz 2016) as opposed to producers and investors. Simply put, rentiers are people who acquire assets and then without any additional effort continue to draw income from them permanently, benefiting also from appreciation in the value of the asset. In finance, such growth and income is highly celebrated and endorsed positively. The word rentier or the phrase financial exploitation are removed from the vocabulary and replaced by 'objective' phrases like risk, value and returns. A lot of investment today has become about wealth extraction as opposed to wealth creation. Huge amounts of money are going into land and property management, or into speculation in financial markets or derivatives (Strange 1986; Das 2011), where there is little effort and money is sucked out from the weak and the powerless – through rent, risk manipulation, price-fixing, pension fund mis-management, property speculation and high taxes on low-income households.

One of the keys to wealth extraction is access to finance. As a simple example, if I buy a house with my own money and it doubles in value after say five years, I double my wealth – a return of 100%. However, if I buy the same house with 90% of borrowed money and it doubles in value after five years, the return on my original investment is 1,100%. The asset is the same and the price rise is the same, so how come the return on investment is so different? Because in one example, I used my own savings to acquire the asset, whereas in the other, I used other people's money, but somehow got the rights to keep all the profits from the growth in values of the asset. The only difference, therefore, is my ability to raise finance for the asset and my cultural willingness to borrow money to finance it. In the first example, I had no access, and in the second, I had good access, so I made a huge return. A major UK government study showed that financially excluded people pay a 'poverty premium' of an average £1,300 every year; they pay more for finance because they are poor and excluded (Financial Inclusion Commission 2015). One may, therefore, ask why it is that access to finance is never discussed or elaborated on in the classroom, and why it is that some people have very good access and others have no access. A discussion on this theme would really engage and empower students.

Speculation is highly addictive. So are drugs and alcohol. In the practice of high finance, these often go hand in hand and complement one another. However, when I raised the question of random drug testing in financial institutions, there was a hushed silence and cover-up (Shah 2014). Finance textbooks are totally silent about the personal and social impacts of speculation or addiction, using phrases like risk-reward, hedging or market timing and value-creation. Finel-Honigman (2010) and Ferguson N. (2012) show how the cultural history of finance is riddled with fraud, gambling and embezzlement, though this is rarely taught in the classroom. At present, there is no discussion about gambling in the business classroom; in fact, the word is not even used and replaced by risk management or maximising return on risk. Given its vast impact on everyday life (Gambling Commission 2017) and ruination of whole families, the personal risks and consequences of gambling are very relevant to a finance class. According to the Gambling Commission, 48% of people surveyed had participated in gambling in the last four weeks. In the process, the addiction of financial risk and denial of its excesses and consequences will come to light, empowering learners to make informed decisions about their future careers. In the case of the global financial crash of 2008, we saw private gambling spill over into national and global catastrophe.

More fundamentally, contemporary finance has totally broken the link between human effort and reward. If managers earn tens of millions of dollars, they are justified in this given the profits they generate for their companies. However, what is the skill and effort devoted to the running of the company, and how much of this comes from the CEO as opposed to the staff who do the day-to-day work? Such issues are rarely discussed in spite of their huge contemporary relevance and topicality. Interdependence is deliberately undermined and ignored in finance. If such matters were discussed in the classroom, they would inform student understanding about the links between business principles and finance theory, and perhaps also help clarify their own ethics and beliefs regarding business conduct. By ignoring or avoiding such basic discussions, we are only giving students half-truths or even lies and fiction.

When Luyendijk (2015) analysed the culture of high finance prevailing in the City of London, one of the world's largest financial centres, he discovered greed, infighting, bullying, addiction, depression, selfishness and constant anxiety. None of this is mentioned in the professional courses and the impression created is that the technical knowledge is all worthy and a key to personal success and happiness. Culture is by definition irrelevant. So is faith or belief, although faith and belief in free, efficient and perfect markets is assumed. Respecting rules and regulations is rarely discussed as a critical quality, and often techniques of legal, tax and regulatory arbitrage are openly discussed or elaborated as normal and profitable. Even in accounting, where learning of rules and standards is a key component for professional training, the conflict of these with ethics or culture is not up for discussion. The politics of the accounting profession and the standard-setting process play a critical role in the outcomes of accounting practice, but little effort is devoted to studying such serious conflicts and contradictions.

One of the best ways to teach culture is through stories – and guess what, most accounting and finance education is totally devoid of stories. Children learn language and words through stories; they remember stories, and novels are read thousands of times more than textbooks. So what is stopping us from bringing finance stories into the classroom? A good story can bring a range of elements together from calculation to risk, value, profit and ethics. It can reveal political and social capital, or the role of education in empowering future leaders to do compassionate acts. And there are a large number of finance stories available to bring into the classroom. Michael Lewis (e.g. Lewis 2008, 2011) is the most famous such writer, but there are also stories on the bankruptcy of Lehman Brothers (McDonald and Robinson 2009) or the history of Goldman Sachs (Cohan 2011) or how the 2008 crash arose (Ferguson 2012). All of these are very enriching and illuminating, and we can even bring positive stories about good accountants and bankers to inspire students to think and act differently. Even better, we can bring some of these people into the classroom to share their stories; it is amazing how many people love coming to teach students at University and share their experiences. Students may also have their own stories and experiences with finance which can shape a useful discussion in class and encourage them to participate in the learning journey. The Academy Award winning film *Inside Job* (Ferguson 2010) has a number of personal stories about how people became victims of financial hubris and fraud, and the devastating consequences of these to their family lives.

The only reason I can think why stories are avoided in the classroom is because they challenge the purely technical interpretations of business and open the boundaries of finance knowledge which experts would rather keep closed. Even where case studies are discussed, they are presented in a very dry and specialised manner, where context and wider factors are fenced off and the interpretation is analytical and particular. Perhaps there should be a whole module on narratives in finance, where students can hear a range of stories about how finance works in practice and its impact on nature and society. There would be a range of ingredients in these stories, from people to products, services, customers, suppliers, lenders and even animals and nature. In a true story, the basics are very important and cannot be avoided, making them impossible to be covered up by restricted or narrow interpretations. These would really expose how narrow the texts of accounting and finance have become. Stories enable students to combine context, meaning, ethics and calculation that are memorable; students could remember the learning long after they leave.

There are many different types of business organisations, not just the corporate or profit-seeking variety where accounting and finance are important. Charities exist to provide a range of services to the needy and often powerless, but they too need to raise funds and account for their income and expenditure. Government and local public organisations need to provide efficient services and collect and manage revenues for these services in a way not dissimilar from modern business. In fact, much of business language has seeped into their management and operations. They too need knowledge and skills in accounting and finance. Social enterprises are often organisations started by entrepreneurs with a purpose other than profit maximisation; they want to provide goods or services to their local communities at affordable prices. Similarly, building societies and mutual credit unions provide financial services, but have very different objectives and criteria from commercial banks. In the teaching of accounting and finance, when we do not mention these organisations at all, we mislead our students' true understanding of the subject. We disable students from understanding the limits of finance, including instances where whole organisations survive without big loans or borrowings and still manage to provide for customer needs in an efficient manner.

The moment we adapt an ethical approach to education, we open the possibility of exploring fundamentals. For example, questions like what is an accounting professional; what is their role and purpose; in what ways are they experts and professionals; how can they be relied upon and trusted; how is their analysis and judgement independent and free from bias? Similar questions can be asked about bankers and other finance professionals. Such discussions in the classroom can help students really understand the links between theory and practice, the kinds of jobs and roles they can aspire to and the consequences of good or bad professionalism. In the process, they begin to clarify their own ethics and values, what they stand for and believe in and why.

Businesses are organised as institutions, and large businesses may seem very daunting and scary to students, especially when they have glamourous buildings and brand names. However, students should be empowered to identify the fundamentals of any business and unlock what it is that helps them profit and grow. Their DNA should be identifiable easily by a graduate student. Banks and accounting firms, or large corporations like Shell or Google or Goldman Sachs, can be simplified in order to reveal their core purpose and methods of operation, and how they meet their objectives and generate profits. They may be huge and global, and even have complex layers of organisation and products, but underneath it all, their purpose and objectives should be relatively clear and observable by a graduate of business. Their gleaming towers and brand names should not be used to allow our students to fear them or to hold them in awe without understanding their motives and purpose. If in the classroom culture and ethics are shown to be important, students are more likely to evaluate the culture of the organisation they choose to work with before they accept a job.

Exercises like these, which are directly relevant to understanding accounting and finance, help students to go beyond the fluff and make their own judgements about business and its agenda. It is hoped that this will reveal that whilst profit maximisation may be a simple overarching goal to teach and promote, its practice can have a wide range of effects on people, society and environment, which are often not measured. Such exercises may also reveal to them the difference between marketing spin and organisational substance, and empower them to make their own analyses and judgements in the future.

I find with many students that even after three years of accounting and finance education, they cannot distinguish between investment and expense – what is paid out for the short term versus the long term and why. They may be able to do the accounting and the calculations but have lost the basic understanding. Given a question about evaluating investments, they may be able to do the discounted cash flow and even come up with the right answer, but they really do not understand what an investment is and why businesses would need to take such decisions. Even risk, a subject core to accounting and finance, is not understood, and the textbooks go straight into its calculation without helping students explore its fundamental nature and the uncertainties and weak assumptions which often lie behind its calculation. Financial risk is socially constructed (Douglas and Wildavsky 1982; Beck 1992) and influenced by culture and values. Such evidence of ignorance and denial exposes how ill equipped students are about the real world, even after several years of business school education.

For most people in life, risk is a lived experience, and in the era of financialisation, it is a significant problem in negotiating life and personal happiness and sustainability. If one has plenty of savings or investments, it is less likely that one will to become homeless or not be able to afford good food, exercise and health care. The contrary is also true – lack of money can lead to poor health, housing and education, reducing life chances. These are the real risks people face and the depersonalisation of finance education is such that they do not occupy any space in the curriculum whatsoever. Similarly, budgeting is a very simple way in which people can manage and monitor their financial risk. Distinguishing between needs, comforts and luxuries can help students understand their financial priorities and live according to their means. Above all, thinking profoundly about risk helps students to think and plan for the future, and anticipate opportunities and misfortunes. It can empower them to deal with the very essence of life and live peacefully and sustainably.

Such ignorance, frauds and mis-understandings about risk led to the last financial crash and will bring us another one unless we help students understand the basics and flaws and limitations of scientific risk measurement and management. In a similar way, in organisations, risk evaluation is often highly charged and political (Shah 2017), yet this is never exposed or discussed in an accounting or finance classroom. In going back to basics, we enable students to see whole truths and perspectives, not just those bounded by what the textbooks or formulae say.

When we look at human history, risk and faith are intimately connected. Prayer was used to manage personal and family risk and misfortunes, and faith often gave people an inner resilience and confidence to accept life's challenges and cope with difficulties. It will come as no surprise that the role of faith is never mentioned in a finance textbook, even when it talks about risk. Similarly, concepts like value and wealth are not objective, and often have many subjective assumptions, ethical and otherwise, which influence how they are calculated, evaluated and used. The ideology that is finance theory pretends that they are entirely objective concepts free from bias and therefore highly relevant to scientific analysis. In fact, this ideology is so perverse that it states at the outset that firms exist primarily to maximise shareholder value. This effectively means that all managers and shareholders are obsessed with selling the firm and cashing in rather than providing a good product or service for the long term in a way which is sustainable for society and the environment. If we continue to teach our students this half-baked truth, then we are perpetuating its religion and encouraging students to be greedy, materialistic and selfish.

In my Jain research on family-owned businesses (Shah and Rankin 2017), I find that most of them are not created for cashing in, but instead they are organically shaped to provide for the whole family, both current and future generations. The ethics of family businesses are often not short-term greedy but long-term manageable and sustainable growth. There is no separation between ownership and management, and often direct ownership leads automatically to responsible business and therefore responsible accounting and finance.

Rather than teaching students straight about large businesses, which are often big, complex and anonymous, I often start by teaching them about small businesses, where the owner is also the manager. I ask them basic questions about why accounting should be important to them and what role would accounting play in their businesses. This creates a kind of intimacy with the subject, and at times students bring in their own experiences of working for such businesses or being customers to such organisations. I also encourage them to explore the wider field of business, which is all around them and something they encounter all the time. The next time you shop somewhere, ask yourself how the business trades, what attracted you to shop there and where its profits and risks could lie. Spark an enquiry, which can then be followed up with research on recent news stories or analyses of their financial performance. When I took a group of first-year students on such a simple field trip, exposing them to a range of local businesses, it was surprising how quickly they could figure out these concepts without any prior knowledge or training in accounting. I know of very few accounting or business lecturers who engage in this kind of activity; in fact, I don't know a single one. The student feedback from such field trips is often positive, and they find the experiences very instructive and memorable.

In Britain, employability is a big thing, and Universities are encouraged to help students find jobs and embark on relevant careers. We can craft teaching in such a way that employability is integrated and they learn at the same time about the subject and job opportunities. Another popular field trip I have organised is to the City of London, one of the largest global financial centres of the world. We do a walking tour of this famous square mile with a guide who is a historian. The institutions we cover include the Bank of England, Lloyds of London, Stock Exchange, and we discover a large number of churches all along the route, showing how faith and finance had been intimately connected. History, jobs and financial institutions are all connected in this one-day experience, which also helps improve student motivation and engagement in class. Organising such field trips and encouraging students early on to question the shops and businesses they engage with automatically helps them think about jobs and opportunities, about different roles of the accountant or the banking professional. Multiple goals can be accomplished by such teaching methods. Employers do not seem big, scary and anonymous, but organisations which have some familiarity with their lived experience, and students have been allowed inside some of them to explore how they operate and manage their businesses. Business field trips act as a career icebreaker and motivator.

Values like trust, honesty, transparency, integrity, accountability and fiduciary duty are common in the business ethics and professional accounting and banking literature. However, students know very little about what they mean in practice, and they mean different things to different people depending on their cultural and family backgrounds. Often the principles are taught in the form of rules and regulations, and, therefore, they are expressed and learnt in an academic way. Students would struggle to translate these concepts into practical actions and judgements.

However, they are key practical principles which are central to the shaping of a quality professional. There are no easy formulae for training students about these values, however. What must be avoided at all costs is a factory-based textbook approach. Small-group discussions and interactive workshops are the most appropriate ways of making a start. Such exercises would encourage students to try to come to terms with their own morality, the reasons behind those views, and the kinds of morality they should aspire to if they want to become respected professionals.

The best way to engage students on this theme is to start by asking them what they understand the principles to mean and then use examples and case studies to illustrate how the need for judgements and character may arise in practice. The choice of these examples should be such that students can relate to them in their everyday lives and experiences. Discussion around these topics would really open the class to dialogue about culture, history, migration, assimilation and common desire to aspire and climb the social ladder. Conflicting principles and ideas may arise, but these conflicts should not be suppressed.

Such dialogues are critical to shaping the accounting and finance professional of the future, but rarely occur in practice within the University. Given what we said in Chapter 1 about a profound moral crisis in business, if we continue to avoid such training, then we will continue to get what we have always got. The morality and character of greed has significant short-term attractions – it gives immediate returns, helps our instant happiness and gratification, gives us a feeling of independence and a measure of success and achievement. If the structures and incentive systems of the organisation where we work are aligned to such behaviour, then we will be encouraged to behave in this way, thinking nothing of the damage to others or the longer-term consequences.

In an environment where students have to borrow money to go to University and graduate with a debt burden, we should not be surprised if society encourages them to be greedy and selfish and to have a short-term horizon in terms of their morality. Debt requires regular payments of cash and incurs penalties for any delay or non-payment. Students could even be tempted to put their knowledge and principles about morality aside when employers offer a high-paying first job. In recent decades, some of the best payers to graduates were banks and professional accounting firms, many of whom turned out to have committed acts of fraud and deceit, and were highly conflicted in their products and services. In the United Kingdom, property prices at present are such that for graduates to get onto the housing ladder, they have no choice but to work for businesses which pay them high salaries and bonuses.

When such discussions are conducted in the classroom, it becomes much easier for students to relate accounting and finance practice to ethics and character in the future. It should begin to help them see the limits of numbers and calculations, and the importance of relationships and culture in giving financial advice and building trust. Another important area where expertise and advice are often needed is risk. Research has clearly shown that a large number of risks are social and cultural phenomenon, especially those relating to finance and money. However, you would not know this if you read a typical accounting or finance textbook. Here, risk is a calculation and a technique of measurement and management. There is a subtle denial of any cultural or moral assumptions in the evaluation of risk. It is all part of the depersonalisation of accounting and finance education.

There are many calls and regulations to encourage modern business to respect nature and act in ways which do the least harm to our environment. However, if we were to study the number of times nature is talked about, let alone experienced, in the modern business classroom, the answer would be very little. If and when it is discussed, the chances are that it would be in an abstract way, where it can easily become a formula to be calculated or a technique to be implemented. However, nature is all around us and much larger than us in size, intelligence, variety and creativity. Engaging with its true essence can be a little discomforting for an accounting or finance student if all he/she is taught is how to profit from nature and thereby exploit it in every which way. Just as economics treats the environment as an 'externality', the business professor treats nature as something on the margins of the mainstream, something that needs mention but does not really affect the core science. This is wrong and unsustainable. In many ways, the textbooks prevent us from genuinely bringing nature into the classroom.

Instead of telling students what to think about nature, we should start by asking them what they consider to be the links between business and nature, and then brainstorm about how accounting and finance might include nature in its theories and techniques. It is possible that a wide range of answers may emerge from such a conversation, but such exercises begin to empower them to be reflective and inspire them to bring their own passions and values into the classroom. With such dialogues, education can make a very deep imprint on the minds of our students. It is likely that in such discussions students may bring up major environmental catastrophes linked to business such as VW and diesel emissions, or Exxon Valdez or Shell in Nigeria. Alternatively, they may even say that there is no link between business and nature; they are separate entities.

Discussing businesses' impact on the environment can help students to see the subjectivity of cost and the assumptions made behind its calculation, which are often not expressed or discussed, yet have a huge impact on the outcome and conduct of business. They would begin to see that what gets measured gets noticed, and what is not measured can be ignored or exploited. The environment can help students see the limitations of account-ing and finance knowledge, and help identify areas where they would need to work with other professionals and experts to develop ways of developing sustainable models of business.

The concept of sustainability is foremost a moral criterion; there is not one but a triple bottom line (Elkington 1999) which needs to include both social and environmental impact. For business to be sustainable, our own values and conduct needs to be such that they are in harmony with nature and respectful of the huge strengths and life-wisdom nature gives to each and every one of us. Once these moral principles become understood, then it is not a big step to engage students in incorporating nature into accounting and finance techniques and practices. In fact, for those who are passionate about this subject, they may discover a new way of looking at accounting and finance which is both interesting and even pioneering.

In my experience of three decades of teaching, business students today have lost connection with many basic elements of life, like trust, relation-ships, nature, and like contemporary business, they have become transac-tional and selfish in their character and conduct. Many have not experienced getting a benefit or helping hand from others and are often scared by the competition in the job market. The anonymity of the job application pro-cess, which is becoming more and more virtual and impersonal, makes them feel that no one respects them or treats them as human beings. If we add large class sizes and a factory-style approach to teaching and learn-ing, with elite researchers thinking big ideas away from the classroom, then even the clever students going to top Universities will feel betrayed.

Even if students are selfish and transactional, it is our role as teachers to act as role models for them and show a different way. Our manners and actions should be caring and sensitive, helping them to see the possibilities of building their own self-confidence. Our teaching methods should be such that students can see personal growth beyond the mark or score they will get at the end of the class, and these should inspire and motivate. We can change our assessment systems to reflect their class participation and the different ideas and contributions they bring to the discussions. Some stu-dents may find the discussions around morality and ethics difficult. How-ever, this does not mean they should be avoided. Instead of drowning them in technical speak, such an approach may empower them towards practical, ethical and meaningful accounting and finance. Through such an approach, they can become agents of change in the character and practice of business.

In summary, this chapter tried to go back to the basics of accounting and finance, exposing its fundamental assumptions and its social construc-tion. In the process, significant flaws in the present system and content of accounting and finance education were revealed, which prevent it from becoming virtuous and sustainable. A holistic approach was charted with links to research breakthroughs which now need to be incorporated into the classroom to bring about fundamental change. Helping students understand the basics and see beyond the technical façade of accounting and finance is critical to building a sustainable society, it was argued. The result would be a richer and more engaging subject, which would empower students to new heights of ability and enthusiasm toward helping to build a virtuous business world.

In the next chapter, we focus on practical examples and methods of implementing a virtuous approach to accounting and finance education. Various people (including me) have already tried and tested some of these with good student feedback. Examples like field trips, stories and narrative, interactive workshops and case studies are illustrated to show how such an approach can enhance the curriculum and improve teaching and student experience. References for different resources which can be used are provided, and creative curriculum suggestions are made to help students get a truly holistic and personal experience of learning. Their life experiences are allowed to be discussed in the classroom instead of being denied or ignored.

3   Reforming teaching
Methods and syllabus

The first two chapters introduced the need for a major shift in our approach to education in accounting and finance, necessitated by the huge global crises we face today. In particular, we showed why ethics and morality have to be at the centre of this renewal and not at the periphery. Given the profound flaws in economic and finance theory, it seems very wrong and misleading to start undergraduate education with these foundations; we must think of a new and very different approach, if we wish to sustain human life on this planet. Such an approach requires students to have a good understanding of philosophy and ethics, of society and politics and of the natural environment, and its intelligence, wisdom and limits. Starting accounting or finance education by focusing straight on business practice and technique without a theoretical or broader understanding of human life, its history and vulnerability would be to deliberately harm the ecosystem and global society. In fact, in elite Universities like Oxford or Cambridge, neither accounting nor finance are offered as undergraduate degrees. The wider implications of such a radical transformation of the primary content and syllabus of business training are to shape a new generation of leaders whose minds are much more open and less technical and instrumentalist.

Examples of subjects that can be taught at the undergraduate level would include history, politics, art, religion, philosophy, ethics, sociology and environmental science. These would introduce students to the diversity of human society and its impact on the planet, as well as the different cultures and world views which prevail. Themes covered should include truth, wisdom, economics, power, environmental restraint, war and plunder, slavery and exploitation, bureaucracy and organisation. Case studies from businesses and their histories from all over the world would reveal the record of business impact and social and environmental transformation. For example, a simple yet powerful fact that the British East India Company went to India to do business but then convinced the king to conquer the country to exploit its riches could reveal the central connection between business and politics.

However, if this case study were shared with a contemporary business studies class, the impact would be very minimal, as they would not have studied history or power and may even think how clever the company was in its profit maximisation.

Universities traditionally used to feign from vocational training and were targeted not at mass higher education but at small groups and class sizes. They were clear about their purpose, which was to inform and inspire, placing theory and not practice at the centre of study and analysis. Now we need to add virtue ethics to the theory urgently. At heart, sustainable development demands a culture change, and reforming education lies at the root of this (Shephard 2015). If Universities were to adopt such an approach for business education, it could shape a different group of finance leaders, who could potentially have a transformative impact on business practice. A large number of senior executives in business do not come from a traditional business studies background, especially those that are creative and inspirational. Perhaps in the final year of such studies, students could be introduced to theories and research in accounting and finance, and the critiques that are being made of mainstream rationalist ideas and practices. It is likely that when they graduate from such a programme, they would be much more broad-minded and capable of leadership positions.

This transformation in the curriculum is a truly radical suggestion and one which will go against the grain of our own jobs and training. My own first degree was in economics and accounting, and this was followed by a professional chartered accounting qualification and then a master's and PhD in accounting. However, if we compare the trajectory of many eminent scholars in the field today, like Christine Cooper, or Anne Loft or Michael Power, their first degrees were definitely not in business or finance, with Mike Power even having a PhD in philosophy. It seems that a theoretical grounding outside business is essential if we are to evaluate and critique it in a profound manner. When we look at contemporary professional training in accounting all over the world (Pehlivanova and Martinoff 2015), none of these wider and older social or philosophical sciences have any role to play in what remains a very practical and atheoretical method of training, but they need to.

In an era of rising unemployment all over the world, and significant competition for quality jobs and education, which is value for money, many students are being forced by circumstances to be instrumental. As a result, business studies are undertaken by students who are motivated by well-paid jobs and towards working in a sector which has a reputation for high earnings, bonuses and profits. An area like entrepreneurship, which is highly competitive, is often portrayed by the media as something great through rags to riches stories, but students embark on such studies with gusto.

Rarely are they aware of the failure rate of entrepreneurs and the number of businesses which never even take off. Often the promise of a lucrative job is enough for business schools to sell their courses, even though they are reluctant to objectively measure the actual impact of their endeavours. When I was recently in India, I saw full-page advertisements with photos of graduates of business schools and a caption showing which big company they are now working for. The employability is a key selling point, demonstrating how pragmatic business schools have become. In such circumstances, how is critique of the very philosophy, politics, greed and methods of business really possible?

One of the world's oldest and largest associations of business schools, the AACSB, recently published 'A Collective Vision for Business Education' (AACSB 2016) which recognised the critical need for ethical leadership and interdisciplinary training. AACSB's research also shows that the public expects business to address a growing array of social and environmental problems, including good health and well-being, strong communities, meaningful employment and a fulfilling life. Corporations cannot just remain selfish and reckless – their reputations have been badly tarnished, and the public can now see through their spin and contradictions. However, when we examine this strategy critically, it has hidden contradictions and refuses to address basic conflicts like those between profit and sustainability or tax avoidance and obeying the spirit of laws. It is aspirational rather than honest or real.

The pace of change in life and technology has meant that education is not a one-off activity, but has to be life-long for people to have jobs, keep them and upgrade their skills for promotion and transition. In the field of accounting and finance, it is possible that an ethical person who builds a reputation and relationships can never be out of a job, especially if they have their own advisory or accounting practice. Their goodwill and trustworthiness will ensure that people will keep coming back to them and recommending them. As such, advisers are needed all the time, as money and finance have become core to human survival, they will likely never go out of business. The disappearance of relationship banking from local communities has meant that the need for local accountants with those trusted relationships is very high.

In a similar way, we can argue that given the changing landscape of society and technology, broad-based ethical education and training in a variety of core social sciences, can become a huge strategic strength later in life. Graduates would now be able to continue their learning trajectory on their own, as they have had a strong foundation in truth, wisdom, society and nature, and can develop critical thinking based on what they read and who they meet. Graduates with such training should be better able to judge right

and wrong, know what they stand for and what they are unwilling to compromise, and negotiate external changes in skills and technologies. They
will develop a deeper self-confidence, self-awareness and self-esteem,
qualities which would themselves be life-long and sustainable. Whilst they
will in time learn rules and techniques to apply to a particular profession,
they are more likely to understand the limitations of these rules and the fundamental assumptions which created them in the first place.

The approach to such teaching cannot and must not be entirely classroom
based. It should be in the society and the environment, and in groups and
reflective meditations, where curiosity is encouraged and sparked. Learners
would develop their skills and confidence in critical thinking through interaction and dialogue, and begin to hear their own inner voice and intuitions.
Even subjects like art, faith and music can be incorporated in these learning
adventures, where deeper questions like the purpose of human existence
and the duty and responsibility we have toward others can be explored.
Field trips and engagement with different elements of nature and society
would help inform this journey of developing a learning foundation at a
formative stage in young people's lives.

In my own teaching, I have done a variety of field trips for students.
A field trip is an opportunity to take them out of the classroom and into
the real world of business. I have taken them inside an accounting firm, to
local shops and businesses, a large supermarket and retail chain, the City
of London and a charity called Citizens Advice Bureau, which helps people
with debt problems (amongst other services). In all these trips, the student
feedback has been very positive and encouraging. They also quote experiences and learnings from these trips in their exams and assignments. A
field trip is an example of a real and memorable experience, one which is
multi-dimensional and where students can make their own interpretation of
what they see and how they understand it. Inside a classroom, the education
ability can be restrictive and devoid of varied experiences.

In an age of cheap access to technology, information and online learning,
there is a global challenge to the physical University – is it really needed,
and if so, what value does it add to the learning experience? Approaches
to learning which emphasise the group experience, and help students to
socialise with one another and develop interaction skills become very critical. These are also invaluable opportunities for reinventing the business
school and developing a niche in the face of stiff competition and too much
similarity of curricula. If we teach about society without helping nurture a
student community on campus, then our teaching will remain abstract and
theoretical at best, and at worst, it will teach students that society is merely
a theory whose time has gone. Similarly, nature is all around us, but often
does not speak our language and can, therefore, be easily ignored in the

learning journey, especially in subjects like accounting and finance. In our teaching, we need to enable experiences with nature which help students to transform their ethics and morality to one which includes all living beings. As teachers and academics, we can no longer avoid practicing what we preach if we are to cultivate and sustain an ethical learning experience. Such a journey would also require us to engage in a deeper exploration about our own purpose in life and how research and teaching helps us to pursue this in a sustainable and morally equitable manner.

It is possible that one reason we are in the current mess with accounting and finance education and training is that there are very few academics who are motivated by ethics in their research and teaching. This was asserted by Arnold (2009) in her analysis of the reasons for the global financial crash – she poignantly asked where we were looking before the crash as there were no advance warnings, in spite of the fact that it was our field of expertise. She asked scholars to clearly declare their ethics in the research they pursue and not hide behind 'post-modernism' or other abstract notions. It is also possible that those intellectuals who are motivated by public service and a respect for knowledge, wisdom and building a fair and just society, are put off by the demands and policing of their research and teaching. As we have seen, the current syllabuses and education curricula and methods are often technical and impersonal, abjectly removing any space for ethical critique and dialogue. How can one teach what one does not believe in? One way is to draw a compartment in one's mind, which separates teaching from research. In this event, the act of teaching becomes a chore, uninspiring to both the teacher and the students, with the result that no one wins. In many parts of the world, business schools give lip service to teaching impact and evaluations, and focus instead on research outputs and performance. The strong research performers are often carefully protected and given little or no teaching, whilst the weak are bullied or thrown out. It is not clear how much the learners know about this inner culture of business education, and attitudes to teaching. One thing is certain – this separation is unsustainable.

It is also possible that such a radical and different foundation for accounting and finance education can not only generate student interest and excitement but also teachers and scholars who are committed to using education to transform society. In practice, it is very difficult to change the ethics of a person, after they have been established in the upbringing and graduate years. However, there are many people in the world, including student idealists and campaigners, who have a clear idea of their purpose, and love the environment and ethics of public education and open enquiry. They can bring a rare spirit of leadership and challenge in business education, and engage all kinds of enterprises and executives who want to shape a more ethical society and sustainable world. Their work would then not just be critical all the time, but actually help build a new vision and bring like-minded leaders to collectively help transform accounting and financial practices.

Research shows that both accounting and finance are deeply political enterprises. However, the politics is rarely discussed in undergraduate training programmes and never in professional training and education. This is misleading at best, and a fraud at worst, if the intention is to empower learners with the truth, and not pedal falsehoods or misleading facts and techniques, disguised as practical skills. One could argue that political negotiation inside an organisation is also a practical skill, very relevant when one is ambitious and wants to climb the career or organisational ladder. By not teaching it, we are actively denying its existence in corporate and professional life.

The political economy of accounting and finance can be taught through sharing research and case studies, as well as by asking learners what they know about corporates and their power. There is a vast body of research on this, both in accounting and in finance. Students are likely to share their experiences of buying and returning goods, of complaining about false bank charges, or how their managers behaved when they worked part-time. Some may even share experiences of how the accountants often come down from their offices to question performance, even though their methods of measurement and evaluation can never be discussed or questioned. There are plenty of examples and case studies of the hubris of high finance, and how deals are done on the golf course or the restaurant rather than through sophisticated debate and analysis. Where the examples and case studies can relate to students' own experiences and with brand names they are familiar with, the message is likely to impact very deeply, and make them reflect on the fundamental natures of the subject they are studying.

Developing students' research and analysis skills are critical to preparing them for a sustainable future, especially in a time of such instability and change. At an undergraduate level, a lot of the syllabus and teaching disables their research and analytical skills, by drowning them with data, formulae and technical complexity – something known as 'cognitive overload'. In such an environment, fundamental critique becomes impossible, and students lack confidence in doing their own research and analysis. They feel disempowered, and if they are asked to do a dissertation or present their own analysis, the most they will do is to lean on other's findings, without even trying to discover something new or different. The fundamental motivation for study and enquiry can be betrayed by the formulaic methods and technical complexity. Such an approach can easily suit those lecturers who want a minimum of fuss or complaint from their students. It can perpetuate the separation and elitism that is common in research-led Universities.

Student response would therefore be either of alienation and disengagement or conformity and compromise towards getting good grades and career progression.

Just as a materialistic and formulaic education suppresses ethics, it also consciously and subconsciously suppresses faith and culture. By not mentioning these in the classroom, the impression both accounting and finance sciences give is that they are irrelevant. In fact, even the research literature on faith and culture in these areas is very sparse, apart from a recent trend in the study of Islamic finance, which has many distinctive characteristics. As we saw in the beginning (Graeber 2014), in the 5,000-year history of finance, faith has played a central role. Similarly, in human history on this planet, faith has played a huge role which cannot be denied or ignored away by a secular education. Given that the practitioners of these sciences are human beings, whether we like it or not, their faith and culture will influence their behaviour and practice.

As an example, one of the oldest faith and business communities of the world are the Jains. They also happen to be one of the most successful in both accounting and finance. Our research study on them (Shah and Rankin 2017) demonstrated their history, ethics and self-regulating character, explaining how such behaviour made them highly respected and trustworthy. Also, leadership in both these fields became very natural for the Jains. The primary ethics of the Jains, of non-violence, non-possessiveness, pluralism and respect for multiple viewpoints, truthfulness and sincerity, have made them who they are today. These ethics are synonymous with the kinds of ethics espoused in this study, and necessary if we are to shape a sustainable society where there is a respect for all living beings.

The experience and evidence of the Jains and their enduring success can be seen as living proof that whilst formulae and techniques can come and go, what endures is ethics and morality. These can be passed on from generation to generation and create a self-regulation of conduct and behaviour which makes it easy for others to trust the practitioners. As business can be a profession where these values are practiced, the Jains have mastered it, and for many people, prudence and enterprise is in the DNA. However, when Jain students go to study business, there are hardly any professors or academics in the whole world who would understand their cultural and ethical heritage. As a result, this uniqueness they bring to the classroom would be denied and suppressed. Even when business ethics is taught as a separate subject, such cultural heritages are denied and a transactional and technical or rule-based approach is adapted.

Teachers can encourage students to share their own cultural theories and approaches to accounting and finance, and ask them to bring stories and examples into the classroom. If they are not aware, this is a kind of homework which could be set. Such an exercise would also show a clear respect for alternative cultures and belief systems and enable them to feel more empowered by their studies. This would make them call their relatives and community members who specialise in these areas, to share their finance methods and inspirations. In this way, a diverse culturally sensitive approach to the teaching of accounting and finance could be developed and adopted. There would be no formula for this, but an active listening and engagement. Members of the class would then discover the genuine cultural and ethical diversity that is in the room, and the variety and richness of experiences and beliefs.

Accounting is now understood to be biased, often making the visible invisible, and creating certain specific visibilities and interpretations of performance and value. Students could be asked to ponder what is real but made invisible by accounting and the limits of what is measured and its inherent bias and prejudices. The numbers may be neat and add up, but what they symbolise or communicate may be much more complex and have serious and potentially permanent income redistribution effects. Executive share options are a classic example of this, hailed in finance theory as a way to align management incentives toward performance enhancement and away from shirking. However, the reality of the impact of such incentives, on behaviour, accounting manipulation and even fraud can be very serious and permanently damaging to the history and future of the business organisation. Simple examples like the denial of human capital, and the treatment of employees as costs rather than shared profit generators, would help reveal the profound political assumptions hidden in accounting. Such exercises can reveal to the students themselves how numbers signify a type of objectivity, but in reality can be subjective and help disguise the fraudulent assumptions behind the calculations.

Reality documentaries and videos can be powerful teaching tools, helping bring the business into the classroom, with true multi-faceted stories which reveal business in all its many dimensions, including accounting and finance. In my classes, I have shown documentaries like the Academy Award winning *Inside Job* (Ferguson 2010) which examines the factors which caused the 2008 financial crash. The film has a whole section devoted to academic hubris and corruption, and how conflicted senior advisers and consultants to regulators had become. They had used their intellectual status to earn high fees and endorse falsehoods and lies about the true performance of banks and whole economies. This can provoke a serious discussion about leadership and ethics, and about the fundamental problems with some of the ideologies of finance. One of my students was so moved by the film that he went to local churches showing their congregations how fraudulent finance had taken over their lives and influenced their predicament. The audiences were shocked as the film demystified the behaviour of bankers and academics, and exposed how they were exploiting millions of ordinary lives.

A picture speaks a thousand words, and a story can last ten or more generations. Modern-day accounting and finance teaching is devoid of both pictures and stories. Its acultural nature wants to suppress stories, as they are too vague and unreal. However, for students, both stories and pictures are very moving and interesting. They make both accounting and finance come alive, and become accessible and understandable. In fact, such approaches make them actually enjoy their learning journey and look forward to the next class, or read and research more into the subject and the current business news and happenings. When motivation is enhanced, the outcomes of the learning become very different. Similarly, technical approaches can demotivate and disempower, leading to outcomes which arise from pain and suffering, rather than joy and understanding. Rarely do they lead to fun and excitement. In high finance, it is often trained mathematicians and rocket scientists who dominate, and they are unable to see beyond their calculations and equations at the real world and the impact of their actions. The technical training prevents them from seeing the subjective, complex and conflicting realities of the world.

Stories are a profound way of engaging students in ethical discussion about accounting and finance. They convey lived examples and experiences, have context and meaning, and can often simplify complex realities, making them easier to understand. They also do not fit into neat boxes and subject classifications, which is probably why they are avoided in contemporary accounting education. Stories can also help research to engage with lived experience and practice, making what is a social science an opportunity for dialogue and creative analysis. There are a huge variety of characters and stories in history in any culture which relate to finance. Also, different cultures have their own current and historical experiences and memories. They simply need to be brought into the classroom. Exposure to a diverse class can also lead to different interpretations of the same story and different questions about ethics and culture in different countries.

Luyendijk (2015) conducted a series of anonymous real-life interviews of various aspects of banking culture in the City of London and published them in a special blog on the Guardian website. The subjects came from a variety of roles inside these institutions, with many from senior positions. The blogs also generated considerable comment and discussion, as so little of this had ever been revealed before, and so many people could identify with the characters in the stories. The aim of these was to unlock something missing significantly in finance training, yet real and highly influential – the way bankers behave and relate to one another. A consistent theme that came from these interviews was a culture of backbiting and back-stabbing, and high internal competition and egoism. This is the opposite of ethical finance conduct, and implies that we should not be surprised by the actions that have come out from these blue chip financial institutions. The culture sets the tone for the character, and in almost all interviews, the participants said very clearly that the buyer of banking services must beware the seller (caveat emptor), who is always out to make a high profit. There is no culture of protecting the customer's interests and financial welfare – something which is a professional and legal duty for bankers. Sharing such true-life stories and case studies of actual behaviour can reveal to students how flawed their images of high finance are, and why the truth is often far from the myth. Luyendijk also found evidence of hidden but rampant drug abuse and alcoholism in the City of London, one of the world's most famous financial centres. Similar stories of accountants in practice would also be revealing about lived experiences and practices, exposing how culture influences behaviour and norms. This would be a world very different from that avowed in the textbooks.

The state/government of any country plays a very important role in accounting and finance. First and foremost, it establishes, regulates and monitors the money and financial system, a core part of all business activity. It also establishes the law and standards which enable banks and financial firms to operate and create products and services, protecting the rights of consumers and citizens more generally. It operates the courts and the police, and either directly provides or regulates the provision of energy, water, transport, education – all critical for businesses to operate efficiently. The state supports the higher education system, often providing the loans and funding for Universities to operate or students to learn. How awful would it be if students were told to forget the very resource that helps them learn or to ignore the infrastructure it provides for their growth and development. It is often much more democratic than accounting firms or financial institutions and is accountable to the public for its actions and their consequences. Taxation, the system by which government collects its revenues to provide public services, depends heavily on accounting and ethical accountants and lawyers, to ensure that rules and principles are obeyed and not disrupted or circumvented.

However, in the teaching of both accounting and finance in a business school, government is entirely excluded as a core institution of commercial life. It is as if business can take for granted all these services, and does not need to care for it or be obligated towards the state. A subconscious impression that such an attitude creates in the minds of students is that government is second-rate and not worthy of study or analysis. In the extreme focus on wealth creation, the state's function is to be exploited rather than respected and obeyed. This is not at all dissimilar to the attitude towards society and the environment. They are there for business use and exploitation, but need no special protection from private business or careful study and analysis from business students. Just as the son of a millionaire often takes money for granted and wastes it, we are doing something similar in business and professional education in both accounting and finance. We are asking students to ignore the state, and exploit it at every opportunity. This is unsustainable and incomplete. In fact, governments are often the largest businesses in any one country. They provide goods and services, collect revenues, employ people and like corporations, are fully accountable to the people. There are therefore many parallels between what students learn from corporate accounting and finance, with public accounting and finance.

A basic course or series of courses about government and its business of running the country smoothly, and helping business to transact is essential. Elements of such a course could cover how government helps businesses find skilled labour and protect its inventions and patents, provide core business services like utilities, law enforcement and tax collection and administration. This would go a long way to give students a truly holistic perspective on business, and how there is a partnership with the state, environment and society in realising its objective of wealth creation and extraction. A lot of core inventions which business relies on today like the internet or satellite technology were first made by government funded research. When such facts and analyses are shared with students, they get a rounded picture of business conduct, resources and stakeholders.

There also exist significant problems and flaws in government accounting which have a big impact on current and future generations (Broadbent and Laughlin 2013). Governments generally do not prepare a comprehensive balance sheet and their income statements are often flawed and inaccurate. One of the core ideas of sustainability is inter-generational equity; society must act so that future generations and their livelihoods are not compromised by the present generation. Finance and financial management lie at the very heart of this problem. Unlimited borrowing today can cause huge crises for the future for example. This can be true both of private corporations and public government. Corporate finance theory does not incorporate inter-generational equity nor do they even consider it. On the contrary, present value calculations enable the future to be collapsed into the present, showing how we can profit from inter-generational inequity. This has calamitous ethical implications, which are never discussed in finance teaching or research. They challenge the very fundamentals of finance.

Thus combining public and private accounting has huge benefits in shaping a very well-informed graduate and professional. It enables students to compare one subject with another, understand the strengths and weaknesses of both and see how different objectives lead to different outcomes. Taxation, which is the subject where the two themes come together, could then become enriched with a much wider dialogue about its role, effectiveness and limitations or creative transformations needed to implement sustainability. Studying social and public enterprises can really empower those students who have a strong civic and public spirit and want to use their skills to help others, not just themselves. Entrepreneurship and good finance and risk management are needed for both types of organisations. It is also very likely that the focus on private business and finance in education has the effect of really damaging the quality and motivation of the talent that is available to public organisations, even though it is most needed. In the United Kingdom, there is a professional body for public and government accountants called Chartered Institute of Public Finance and Accountancy, which often struggles to recruit graduates from business degrees.

Jain monks and nuns live with zero finance – they are not allowed to own anything or carry any money. This raises questions about how they live and where they find food, housing, health care and security. It is a fact today that there are Jain monks and nuns all over India, including the busy cosmopolitan cities of Mumbai and Delhi who live in this way. It would be interesting for students to meet them and ask them questions about what it feels like to live with zero finance. Shah and Rankin (2017) explore this in detail giving examples of how sustainability and interdependence are embraced by such ethical living.

A key component of both accounting and finance is law, rules and regulation – both accounting practice and the licencing of banks and financial institutions is controlled and closely supervised. However, this is rarely taught properly to undergraduates. An ethics-based teaching approach could lay a really important foundation for students to understand the fundamental meaning of regulation, its costs and benefits, objectives and outcomes. At a very simple level, where leaders and professionals have a high personal standard of morality, they become self-regulating, saving their employers and the government lots of money. If they see something is wrong, they will not take a part, and even challenge authority for the sake of truth and fairness. However, we have an elaborate system of laws and rules to ensure people behave morally, and this costs a lot of money to enforce. Enforcement and policing of personal behaviour is very complicated, and there is a lot of evidence that people use corporations to hide their illicit activity, and often get away with it as a result. Offshore tax havens are a classic example of this. The difference between laws and norms could be taught here, and students could learn how ethical behaviour brings tremendous value to business and society. It is not just a nice thing to do, but has huge business, economic and social implications. Consumer protection laws try to protect consumers from fraudulent finance as an example and professional monitoring polices protect professional conduct.

Teaching an ethical approach to accounting and finance requires students to understand what unethical accounting and finance looks like, and what the consequences are of such behaviour, personal or otherwise. Many bankers only realised the huge pain and adversity created by their actions after the 2008 financial crash, by which time remorse and regret were useless as the damage had already been inflicted. There are plenty of real-life case studies, both present and historic, of accounting and finance failures which led to corporate and sometimes wider economic crises. These are rarely studied in the pro-business school of education, as they bring shame to the profession and its reputation. However, if the aim is to expose the whole truth, then they comprise a very important field of study and analysis.

Personal reprimands from dishonest or fraudulent deeds can also be useful in helping students understand the consequences of bad actions. In the magazine *Economia*, there is often a page which lists all the disciplinary actions against members of the Institute of Chartered Accountants in England and Wales. These could be discussed and read out in class to show stories of penalty and misdemeanour. Very rarely are partners in the Big 4 accounting firms prosecuted in this way, showing how even the profession targets the small people and the powerless. These penalties can be from professional bodies or the state, and may even lead to imprisonment, although sadly in business, this has become relatively rare. Bad publicity can also damage professional reputations and in an age of social media, this is not easy to prevent when one commits wrongs. In an era of constantly increasing regulation, and changes in regulation, there are serious challenges to operating as an independent professional as the costs and burden of keeping up may prove unaffordable to a sole practitioner in accounting. Sadly, it is a fact that not all laws and regulations improve ethics – some argue that they actually help lawyers and accountants to profit from advisory work, rather than creating a more ethical society.

Sustainable education and mass education are a contradiction in terms – an oxymoron. The ideas expressed throughout this book call for a personalised philosophy and approach, attuned to the local student market, or international student audience, if the business school can attract such students. The tremendous focus on profit maximisation, which is at the heart of most business schools (see, e.g., Warwick 2014), is also a folly as it contradicts the very philosophy espoused in this book. Their own model of operation must be crafted in such a way as to be patient and sustainable, where both faculty and administrators work in a respectful and caring way, and give quality time to their learners. The design of the architecture could also be made fitting to the ethical purpose, and nature could be allowed into the building in a creative and inspiring way to remind students of its awe and capacities. I know of one recent international University who have completely redesigned their business school with this in mind, although there is no change in the culture or ethos of the institution or the content of the courses. As a result, even this formula or imposition can fail miserably if there is no humane backbone. For a large part of the business education world, we must understand that international students are simply not there – this is because their colleges do not attract overseas students. However, this does not mean that they do not wish to innovate or develop specific niches. Here are some ideas about how this can be done.

Trust, social capital, relationships, respect for nature and biodiversity, respect for students from different sexes, abilities, classes and beliefs and a lack of greed are crucial to the implementation of an ethical teaching approach. These values can be encapsulated by a niche approach, where the aim is not to recruit masses of students, but to cultivate a different learning and teaching culture, and provide a unique learning experience. Patience also needs to be practiced as it is a core part of sustainability and helps create a long-term education agenda. In an era of life-long learning, such an approach can lead to greater student loyalty and commitment to the institution, long after they graduate, and may even lead to continuing streams of revenue from the students.

The faculty for such a business school need to be selected not only on the basis of their qualifications and publications but also on their ethics and virtues. Such a business school can develop solid local relationships with like-minded businesses and organisations. It can also become a platform for doing research which helps identify and promote good examples, and strategizes and trains leaders to build sustainable accounting and finance enterprises. When students are heard, and their experiences and voices respected, they become engaged and see the learning journey as not only one of certification but also an approach which really opens the mind and heart. Its effect is much deeper than a brand name or a textbook can ever convey. It is very likely that the behaviour of the faculty will spark high levels of motivation and engagement among students, and they may automatically become brand ambassadors for the school and its mission.

Art and creativity should also lie at the heart of such an approach and not at the margins. The curriculum could be shaped in such a way that nature and interactions are allowed to inspire brainstorming, and really whacky and out of this world ideas are debated. A lot of entrepreneurship is born in this way, against the status quo, and the business school, with a clear vision of nurturing sustainable finance, can facilitate this. Innovation hubs have become common now, but so many are inspired by get-rich-quick myths and greed, that they go completely against the grain of this book. Instead, we should try to shape hubs which are about social enterprise and environmental protection, where we can use organisations to build and sustain an ethical society.

Specialisation in accounting and finance at undergraduate level is common and popular; in fact, it is one of the most popular business degrees in many parts of the world. However, as accounting and finance are different aspects of business, there must be a foundation of what business is about and its variety and diversity laid before the specialisation is attempted. I recall when practicing as an auditor, a common criticism I heard from clients – audit staff never understand their business and they have to repeat this training every year when new staff come on audits. Different industries have different risks and opportunities. Revenue sources and costs may differ from one industry to another like say between banking and manufacturing. Students need to be able to discern these differences and their implications for accounting and finance. This diversity of business practice can be fascinating for students to study and analyse, and they can be asked to connect with common brand names and their risks and methods of operation.

I find that even graduates of business do not really understand the power and potential of institutions, and the DNA of organisations. They may spend a lot of time understanding processes, systems and structures, but somehow get lost in the detail and fail to see the big picture. I would like graduates to feel empowered to do their own research into a job they are applying for, and discovering what the core purpose is, and how the business is organised to deliver the core purpose. This does not require a lot of technical skills, but does need solid training about institutions and the huge influence they have on society. It can also help them do well in the job interview, and ask relevant questions. Culture is very important for any incoming employee to understand, but may not be reflected in the company brochures and the spin. Our teaching could help students build a basic checklist about how such cultures can be discerned and the way this compares with the students' own expectations. At my University, we have a first-year course in financial markets and institutions, which helps them develop a basic understanding of the different products, jargon and variety of firms which occupy this space. Students find this fascinating, and I think it works very well. It helps create a foundation from which other ideas can be developed. However, very few Universities which teach accounting and finance have any module on institutions at any level. The theories and techniques can really disengage them from the real world of business and finance if we are not very careful.

Just as maps are needed to help understand the landscape, contours and important places and buildings in an area, students could be asked to build an accounting and finance map of their local area. Mapping technology has really evolved and can help in identifying locations, even drawing and colouring maps to reveal layered truths and realities. Mapping is an excellent way of making the invisible visible, and creatively showing where activity lies, jobs are located and help identify the variety of businesses and institutions which populate the accounting and finance landscape. It can also show the types and levels of specialisation, the variety of risks and services and the levels in which skills are exchanged through networks and engagement. A University, if it is well established locally, could play a significant role in engaging with the local business community, and the map can make the impact visible and identify gaps where work needs to be done. Such an exercise can help students learn about context in the subject area and the influence of human activity and institutions in providing core services and local needs. It can also reveal gaps where entrepreneurial opportunities can lie.

Complexity helps significantly in generating students and getting them to come to our courses and learn from us. However, complexity can also be a tool for making simple things complex, and this is especially true in both accounting and finance. The last chapter was devoted to the basics of accounting and finance, and why they are critical to learning. The textbooks often do not help simplify things because they are written by experts who have forgotten what it feels like to be lost and confused, and who are keen to display their knowledge and authority. We, therefore, need to be very careful about the textbooks and readings we select and give to our students, and make extra efforts to ensure that they do not undermine their confidence or put them off the subject altogether, as so often happens. Basics should not just be mentioned at the start, but regularly repeated and reinforced for students to see the linkages. For teachers, this can and often is a real challenge, but I find it very beneficial because it helps me to stay grounded and be able to connect the teaching material to contemporary events which affect personal and family lives.

There is a specialised aspect of highly mathematical and technical finance which can give trained mathematicians very high-paid jobs and rewards; inside banks, they are known as 'quants'(West 2015). Relative to the total number of accounting and finance jobs, the total number of quants required is very low. Often they are trained outside of business in areas like physics or mathematics, with advanced degrees even PhD's. However, inside banks, they are often misfits (Luyendijk 2015) and find it difficult to communicate their research to managers and compliance officers from non-quant backgrounds. High complexity requires very good communication skills, and it is not always easy for both to go together, as often the very complexity undermines simple communication. In a similar way, risk is a key component of high finance and needs to be measured and monitored accurately, and often experts may know how to calculate and analyse, but forget the very dimensions and nature of risk and uncertainty (Shah 1997b). There is a significant need for balanced training between concepts and technique, and striking the right tone is never easy and gets more difficult the more sophisticated the science.

Jargon often is unregulated and has multiple meanings and interpretations (Graham 2013). These can also vary from country to country and become more complex as a result of different local languages and customs. Like most professions, in accounting and finance, we absolutely thrive on jargon. I encourage students to have a specialist dictionary by their side so that when they are stuck, they can decipher the meaning and move on. What is really important to convey is to ensure that they do not allow the jargon to overwhelm their basic knowledge and understanding, or even worse, demotivate their studies altogether. What can be equally liberating for them is to use simple everyday words to explain concepts and analyses. For example, explaining that profit = sales − costs and coming back to this when having advanced discussions about social responsibility or environmental accountability can really help them gain confidence and understanding.

Communication skills are highly emphasised by employers, both in accounting and in finance. Professional bodies put a strong emphasis on this, saying that in recruiting, they often take the technical skills as a given. However, it is not easy to give these to students in business courses, partly because of the technical nature of the content. Jumping from technical calculation and work to human engagement and communication is not easy. Unless students are taught the limitations of technique and the wider context and subjectivity of accounting and finance, they will find it difficult to communicate outside their disciplines. They also need to practice such communication, and the classroom can enable them to do so through group projects and presentations.

Good communication of technical information to a non-technical clientele or audience can be a huge practical strength in career progression. The accountant or banker needs to learn how to make his/her products and services understandable to different audiences. Communication is a learned skill which requires time, perseverance and lots and lots of practice. Students could be taught, however, to learn to value communication skills and improve their essay writing, report writing and presentation skills through assignments and group projects. They could explain the challenges of communicating to a non-financial audience and be given tasks which require them to do so, helping them to improve their fundamentals. Examples from real life of the different types of communication undertaken by accountants and bankers, and the different levels of impact and engagement that result from these could make for a very lively class. In fact, accounting is also a language of financial communication, with all its strengths and weaknesses. Students could be asked to critique an annual report from its communicative ability and come up with new ways of communicating, which are more ethical and understandable.

Research emphasises primary data and evidence as a means of learning and testing theory. However, rarely do I see lecturers emphasising field learning in spite of the fact that business is all around the students, and they encounter it every day sometimes several times a day. A simple checklist could help them learn each time when they visit these organisations, with simple questions such as the following:

- What is the main business activity?
- How are profits generated?
- What skills are required in managing the business and monitoring the performance?
- What are the business risks and opportunities?
- What role does good accounting and measurement play in the efficient running of the business?
- What is the role of finance in supporting the business activity?

Such an exercise can help them not only to 'think' commercially but also understand and interpret the business, and hone their skills of observation, interpretation and analysis. These are critical to making a good accountant or financier. They are also excellent research and learning skills, and likely to be very memorable in the exam room.

An early open dialogue about ethics and virtues can be very helpful in encouraging learners understand what they value and where they stand in terms of wealth, society and the environment. Such dialogues could uncover a sense of satiation from a certain level of income and wealth, rather than the unlimited greed that is often celebrated and encouraged in the business school. It could also expose to one another how similar or different their moral positions are and can be an excellent foundation for analysing the values of accounting and finance, and what distinguishes a professional from a tradesman or even a businessman. Ideas about knowledge, standards, service and satisfaction and contentment may emerge from such a dialogue. The class could even explore the ethical motivations behind enrolling on this course and what having clarity about this can reveal to them as students. It would lay a very important foundation for an ethical journey, which could be periodically replenished through the specific courses studied, and there could be an exit audit to see how their ethical positions have changed after enrolling on the course. Awareness and knowledge can help change behaviour, especially at a time when people are young and exploring truth, wisdom and the purpose and meaning of life. To avoid having such dialogues at University is to prevent them from developing holistically.

Trust is another ethical quality critical to both accounting and finance. However, to discuss it academically has no impact. It needs to be discussed in a way that is relatable and personal. Here are questions I would raise in a class on trust:

- What does it mean?
- What are the benefits of trust?
- Why is trust important in business and finance?
- What is lost if there is no trust?
- How can trust be created?
- What is the meaning of integrity?
- How can a person 'walk their talk'? What prevents them from doing so?

This can open a very important window into the meaning of the word 'accountability' and how its practice is aimed at improving trust through transparency. Why should accounts be accurate and reliable? Who wins from accounting fraud, and who loses? What is the difference in information needs for a business which is managed by the owner and one which is managed by delegated agents? These are questions which can get to the very heart of fundamental issues in accounting and finance, but are rarely used in the classroom or even discussed. Technical and formulaic approaches overshadow deeper engagement and analysis whose transformative effect can last a long time after students graduate.

Such approaches can shape a solid and strong foundation for later more advanced themes like auditing, corporate governance and reliability of accounting information. Often students study a whole course in auditing without having a clue as to what it means fundamentally and why it is needed. Explaining the trust gap between shareholders and managers can make a useful foundation for this, justifying the importance of good auditing and financial reporting. Students could then also reflect further upon what good means in terms of trust; hopefully, we would get answers like accuracy, timeliness, reliability and honesty. Students could be made aware of the fact that the methods by which accounting and financial numbers are generated are not always objective or standardised, and there can be considerable scope for changing the 'formulae' to get answers that management wish to convey to the markets. This will help them see the link between ethics and calculation, and further examples of how even auditors can be compromised by conflicts of interest would help them see the bigger picture connecting trust and professionalism.

Whilst capital is constantly discussed in both accounting and finance, there is never any mention of social capital. We know from much research in the social sciences that it exists, is valuable and can have a significant impact on an economy and society. Social capital is the networks and relationships which exist to support a village, a community or a whole town or city and even a country. A professional body is an example of a social network which has significant resourcefulness, power and influence. But there are many others cut across lines of faith, kinship, school, clubs and societies. In fact, there is a huge emphasis on networking for business success, and what is really meant here is that your contacts and relationships can really help you get started and sustain your enterprise. However, its monetary value is not measurable, and therefore ignored. Social capital plays a key role in educating students about ethical finance, and needs to be discussed in the classroom. It is an extension of trust and proves how relationships can often be much more powerful than money or knowledge.

Financial risk is often experienced very personally, yet rarely discussed or debated even in a business finance class. Examples of this could be student loans, home mortgages, unemployment and hardship, budgeting and income management, prudence and expenditure control. There are plenty of true-life stories where these things have failed for people and transformed their lives, even breaking up families and leading to homelessness and even mental health crises. There is a tendency in business education to discuss only the success stories, but the failure stories are equally instructive too. And when we look at these at a personal level, they really hit home into students' lives and aspirations, and help them to engage with the deeper meaning, measurement and management of risk. It can make what is abstract very real and what is ignored or excluded from analysis highly suspect and questionable. Analysis of risk can help students become critical and reflective about finance. A mortgage is a long-term commitment, and taking it on can lead to a burden which needs to be managed carefully and can be very costly if one is unable to keep up repayments. Students may even come to understand how some aspects of finance are not very far from a willing slavery, where the chains are accepted willingly with the hope of rising house prices, and the master is not visible. This can start a profound ethical discussion about property and inequality.

Savings and investments are an important cushion against risk, but again not discussed in class from a personal perspective. Students need to understand the value of savings and the personal benefits of investments if they have any hope of negotiating life after leaving the classroom. Savings shape a culture of safety and prudence, where there is a concern for the future and a desire to take control of one's life, rather than allow credit card or debt companies to control it. Investments are methods of earning regular returns and may also provide capital growth. Showing these as an equation in a present value calculation has much less impact then helping students to see how good investments can improve their lives and those of their families and relatives. Now the subject becomes real, and the calculations become understandable.

It is said that the only things certain in life are death and taxes. In both accounting and finance, the impersonal nature of the sciences mean that death is never discussed. Just like people, even jobs and businesses can die. Death has real financial consequences for the family one leaves behind. Death also has the possibility of sharpening our sense of purpose and meaning, something which perhaps contemporary business does not want us to think too deeply about. Death is also the comma (and not the full stop) which helps us considerably in thinking about and living sustainably. If we never died, there would be no future generations to worry about. Facing and talking about the reality of death, and its financial consequences can help bring risk and prudence to life in the classroom. And everyone would have some experience of death in the family, so they will have a lot to say. It can really make the subjects come alive.

Respect and tolerance are virtues increasingly discussed in the global arena due to significant awareness about different people and their habits and abilities, and the need to live in peace and acknowledge their human rights. Racism is also a continuing issue and something often suppressed on campuses from discussion, at least in Britain, where it is seen as too sensitive. However, cultural diversity is a reality, and we have to learn to accept and work with different cultures. Theorising and intellectualising about diversity is not enough; it needs to be discussed and related to practical matters of business and finance. Talent and skill can come from any gender or race, so why is there a glass ceiling in UK boardrooms of even international corporations? Is there a hidden belief that only certain people possess the necessary skills for leadership? How can one trade globally when leaders are mono-cultural? Where is the cultural intelligence in the boardroom which can be applied to its business and financial relationships? Such questions can lead to healthy debate, especially if the class is diverse.

Accounting and finance at first sight appear to be beyond race and discrimination, although underneath the surface, there is evidence of how jobs and the professions are not as equal as they might seem (Edwards and Walker 2009). We cannot avoid addressing issues of equality and human rights if we want to get to the roots of ethics. Similarly, conversations may also go into faith and belief, something which is completely avoided in contemporary accounting and finance, which see them as secular and progressive. However, they are an important reality for many people, and to deny belief is to avoid an ethical conversation from connecting to personal life and practices. In fact, one could argue that faith is a very important foundation for morality, and for many believers, it creates a self-regulating mechanism for ethical behaviour and conduct. Such people already have principles and virtues, and a class in ethical finance can build on this knowledge and experience instead of ignoring or denying it. Accepting that ethics are primarily about living character and attitudes, which can never be fully taught in the business classroom, it is important that student faith is acknowledged and respected.

The buy-now-pay-later mentality is facilitated by finance and operates in personal life as well as in business. It leads to a cultural transformation in our lifestyle which can be permanent, making us addicted to finance and dependent on it. However, this behaviour is completely antithetical to sustainable living, because here we need to worry about the future and restrain the debts we leave behind for future generations. Our attitude should be to buy now only if we can pay for it now and then also only if we need it. There must be a clear understanding of need and affordability, which an economy driven by debt and consumerism does not want people to understand. However, it is imperative that in our teaching we help students understand these basics and see how important they are to their personal lives and happiness and the long-term survival of the planet.

Another practical way to make the whole educational and learning experience real is to organise a peaceful and reflective retreat with students where we go away from the town or the University into a tranquil place. The natural environment, with a relaxed space for bonding and interaction, may engender a deeper reflexivity among students and a desire to make a difference in the world. The discussions could range from life goals to professional ethics, meaningful business and cultivating character and discipline in life. It could help place the richness of learning and wisdom as central to their character development and career, and build a community of learners who may support one another in future.

The next chapter brings together the main insights of this book and explains how such reforms could benefit the teachers and providers of business education. It highlights the virtuous and financial rewards which may accrue and the joy of teaching where students and their experiences matter. The chapter explains the benefits of creating an environment where students become truly empowered and motivated to embrace sustainable business, accounting and finance. The outcomes of such educational programmes are likely to be sought after by business as it tries to change and adapt to the needs of a peaceful and harmonious society. Both students and teachers would be much more empowered in the process and motivated to make a difference.

4 The benefits of a glocal revolution

Throughout this book, the approach we have adopted is to make ethics personal for both the teachers and the students. We have taken a holistic approach with a clear and declared bias towards equality, human rights, animal and environmental protection. Readers are being asked to be virtuous and reflective about their work and its impact on learners. The analysis has been deliberately normative and not positive or value-free (if anything can ever be so pure). Sustainable business and finance are the urgent needs of today, something to be studied, theorised, debated and, most importantly, LIVED. The science is clear, but the practice is often commercialised and politicised, and one key to reforming practice is to reform education. Neoliberalism has given the excuse for society to not engage with personal beliefs and ethics, but in the process, it has also imposed materialistic and selfish ethics which have led to this moral crisis. Education systems have also suppressed culture, morality and identity, and these need to be resuscitated and revived for a truly sustainable finance.

This also means there is a need to reform the content of the teaching, the theories and the evidence promulgated and the methods adopted. The real world is important and should not be separated from the classroom. Therefore, personal beliefs, customs and experiences matter hugely. Similarly, local business practices, cultures and realities also matter for education to really connect, inspire and transform the student experience. The findings of global research are also relevant in guiding us towards what is ethical and sustainable in business, and how accounting and finance need to reflect this in its curriculum.

Specialisation in education often makes a subject very technical and its language, concepts and jargon, inaccessible to ordinary untrained people. This is valuable to the expert or the person who wants to learn the expertise as it can generate demand, jobs and power. In the journey towards professional status and qualification, technique comes to supercede ethics, virtues and a sense of the big picture: how are my work and actions impacting on wider society? Do I create jobs or destroy them? What about the families and communities I may hurt by my actions? If I don't see them, how am I going to see the suffering? Also, there may be a complex chain of personal action and social and environmental impact which I may not understand or even not want to understand.

Chapters 1 and 2 exposed the profound problems with modern accounting and finance, which relate to the basic assumptions and theories on which the sciences have been built. Economic theories have been individualistic and, therefore, impersonal, even when we know that no man is an island. Said (1993) explained that professional expertise leads to narrow-mindedness, where we lose sight of history, politics, context, ethics, nature, institutions, networks, knowledge limits, etc., and instead can become arrogant, selfish, protective and deeply insecure and even aggressive. This creates a big dilemma for accounting and finance education as both supply and demand have tended to be technical and jargon-filled. The kinds of leaps of thinking and imagination called for in this book are, therefore, very difficult if one is already deeply immersed in these professions.

This book is creative and constructive, helping readers to see the possibilities of change and transformation that exist within accounting and finance. One of the great blessings of teaching in these areas is the high student demand, which is rare in many disciplines and declining; examples of this include theology, history, sociology and even economics. This demand also supports our jobs, research and scholarship, and we must not forget the opportunity it has given us for reflexivity and critique of the discipline. The examples and creative ideas presented in Chapters 2 and 3 have the potential to make for a very enriching student experience. These ideas may even encourage young people who are passionate about society and the environment to consider our field as an important career prospect, something that they would otherwise have dismissed. The kinds of approach we have taken in this book require learners to have a sense of concern for nature and society, and an inclination towards virtuous living.

The ideas presented here can lead to revisions of individual courses as well as reconstruction of whole degree programmes at undergraduate and postgraduate levels. They also require revision of the culture and ethos of the business school and its methods of teaching and profit-making. Field trips require planning and networks, and force the teacher to engage with living businesses and institutions. Similarly, creative classes may mean less reliance on the textbook and a greater need to generate unique teaching materials and topics. For many teachers, this can be hugely demanding if there is little time to plan, prepare and execute. Also, in the short term, the rewards for such innovation may not be easily available. What this book is asking for is a change in the leadership of the business school and a commitment to not do what we have always done, but to teach what will nurture a peaceful and sustainable future for all of us.

This transformation should be seen by the teacher or academic as an opportunity and not a sacrifice. It will help us to clarify our own values and moral positions, and relate these to the content of our teaching and education. It will help us become clear about the basics of the subject and ensure our foundational assumptions are consistent. It can transform both our teaching experience and the learning journey of the student such that both get connected and inspired by a wider social and environmental challenge. Instead of forcing us to separate our teaching from our research, and regard one as a chore and the other as a priority, we can use this philosophy to show our institutions how both are important and interdependent in a holistic planet. Above all, such an approach can give us a heightened sense of meaning and purpose, something that can really inspire us to newer depths in research and teaching. We can rise from being classroom transmitters to role models who nurture and cultivate future leaders and breed a caring and responsible finance. In this way, our knowledge and wisdom can become truly sustainable.

Often students are not only coming to learn at University but also to look for positive and inspiring role models. At primary school, a teacher is a very important role model to children. I remember my daughter always play-acting like a teacher at home. When a teacher is kind, caring and helps learners widen their skills and horizons and gives them an opportunity to transform their life, they will not forget it. Selflessness always ripples far and wide when it is genuine, and there is no calculation of return or reward. Not only will students remember what they learnt but also what they have seen in the teacher models of good and professional behaviour and ethical conduct, which they could emulate. In an age of anonymity, where young people have few relatives or community or faith loyalties, the teacher could potentially inspire them to conduct which is fair, ethical and sustainable. In reforming business education, we also need good role models who inspire and motivate ethical thinking and behaviour.

Such an approach can bring sustained economic and financial rewards as the institution which provides such learning experiences becomes sought after, both by students and employers. It would also become a magnet for teachers who want to bring transformational thinking into the classroom and help improve society. When cultural diversity is embraced, the market will become truly global, and the learning experience will also feel inclusive and culturally sensitive. The business school would then become a place of bridge building and deep enquiry about building a sustainable future. In the process, a brand and reputation can be developed, which may also attract philanthropic funding.

The practice of business research and education in the modern world is that it is segregated and often colonised. Europe and North America dominate the field, with Australia also having an influence, but Asia and Africa are relatively far behind apart from a few exceptions. A majority of countries in the world do not have strong research cultures or traditions, are disempowered by the dominance of the English language and do not have access to high quality research training, resources and guidance. Professional bodies and textbooks developed in the West have a huge influence on the education of the whole planet. Its reforms can, therefore, also have a very large and global impact if the West takes its educational responsibilities and accountabilities very seriously. There seems to be a vacuum in global leadership of sustainable business education, and accounting and finance lie at the heart of this vacuum.

The dominance of the intellectual tradition in accounting and finance is therefore mainly white and mostly male. As competition in research is globalised, the same pool of talent is pursuing the top journals, indirectly pressuring writers to use western theories and research methods in their analysis. Academics, whilst being critical of this increased policing, also perpetuate it by saying that we are obligated to follow the rules and appease our masters. Risk in teaching and research is often not tolerated as a result, giving us the outcomes we see: a narrow and parochial teaching factory. What suffers hugely as a result is the diversity of theories and data, and the wide variations in local approaches to business and finance, which very rarely come to light. My own experience of writing one such book about the Jains took 30 years to research and compile (Shah and Rankin 2017). It required a long time to build the confidence and cultivate the intellectual standards demanded in the West. There is often little encouragement and support for such work, and the burden of proof is overwhelmingly on the minorities. In spite of our wisdom and insights, we are often on the back foot. The intellectual colonisation and imperialism in business education is a very real experience for many. Not all are able to challenge and critique it, or have an influence on the curriculum and methods of teaching, especially in developing countries.

If the West dominates the research and teaching content, then it is important to understand its history and cultural biases. Large professionally managed modern businesses and global accounting firms as we know them today are a creation of the West. The separation between shareholder and manager is also a deeply western idea, and so are the creation of professions and the rules and laws for business and markets. Less than 100 years ago, many countries in Europe, were busy colonising the world and conquering its peoples for private profit and national advantage. Sustainability was not even heard about, let alone theorised. Nature and cultures were there to be controlled and civilised by the superior white peoples. The British East India Company was largely responsible for the colonisation of India and China – the two largest countries in the modern world. Greed is therefore embedded deeply in the cultural and institutional psyches of these countries, and it is not fair or trustworthy if they now turn around and say business should be more ethical without acknowledging this violent history. Similarly, for a long time, nature was seen as something to be owned and exploited in these cultures, so they do have profound difficulties in truly embracing sustainable ethics where man is a trustee of nature rather than its master. It seems unfair that the West now controls the world's theories and knowledge about science, technology, faith, society and enterprise. This may be and some argue is a continuation of colonisation and control by other means, often more subtle, sinister and, therefore, more powerful. The multi-national corporations, the largest plunderers of modern society, are a creation of the West. They are now everywhere and nowhere (when it comes to taxes and social responsibility). Giant corporations are keen to exploit local markets and cheap labour, with profits squeezed and transported as 'returns' to Western shareholders and investment funds for their comfort and lazy rewards.

Earlier chapters have made very strong claims about teaching and research in accounting and finance; a lot of the theories are partial or fictitious and harmful to society and the planet. Their premises and foundations are flawed, and the lack of interdisciplinary teaching makes the subjects very narrow, technical and limiting in their education potential. These foresights are very critical and challenging for scholars, teachers and professional bodies. There is also a sense of urgency required and demanded by the planet, which can make all of us feel uncomfortable, especially if we have a lot of vested interest in our teaching and research. Some of the reforms needed to implement these ideas are not just personal, but cultural and institutional, which may be beyond the control of the reader. They are also political.

Throughout the book, we have emphasised the personal as being a key to transformation; virtuous professionalism is needed. This means that ethics is about living, which is much more important than learning. Student or teachers bring their own values to the classroom, and whatever they are, they need to be acknowledged and discussed. Research and science has taught us about different cultures and philosophies from all over the world, and about the unsustainability of greed, selfishness and materialism. These facts need to be openly discussed in the classroom if business ethics education is to have any lasting impact. Sadly, such discussions are avoided in many parts of the world, if business ethics is taught at all.

Just as the personal is important, so too is the local. Whilst we know that institutions, politics, networks, markets, corruption and elites matter, such facts are rarely discussed in undergraduate classrooms even in the West, let alone other parts of the world. In fact, we could even argue that the impersonal business science of the West is designed to undermine the true nature of business and cover-up for its misdemeanours. Similarly, in each country of the world, there is often a diversity of languages and cultures, religions and beliefs, urban and rural businesses, and students need to be taught this diversity in the classroom for their studies to be relevant and meaningful. They would be able to relate to some of it directly and learn new things, but to ignore it in favour of a 'smart international textbook' is to suppress their own wisdoms and experience. Cultural intelligence and sensitivity are very important to modern business (HBR 2016), and accounting and finance education can reflect this to everyone's benefit. As an example, Shah (2007) explains the benefits of this diversity for people living in the United Kingdom.

Critical thinking and self-evaluation of ideas and concepts is key to student growth and understanding in any discipline. In many parts of the world, the teacher and the textbook are Gods, and there is no desire to challenge or question such authority. If on top of this we add the barriers of speaking and articulating a critical view in a language different from one's own, this becomes very tricky, impossible even. The dominance of English as the language of instruction and research in accounting and finance also has the effect of silencing third world voices. Scholars from many different parts of the world who may be brilliant but cannot be articulate in English are penalised.

In addition, as we have already seen, numbers and calculations seem definitive and unbiased, and so many people easily get fooled by them. It is also possible that in many parts of the world, the very students drawn to accounting and finance studies are already very technically and mathematically oriented, so they lack the critical faculties needed to study these disciplines in an ethical context. There is a kind of self-selection bias, which makes greed easier and sustainable thinking and behaviour harder. The beauty of numbers is that they are understandable in any culture. Perhaps that is why accounting and finance education has transported so well globally; it does not require much cultural training. Calculations and techniques can be easily memorised, learnt and replicated, but cultural and ethical analysis is trickier. Also, in the exam room, essays are much harder to write than calculations for such people, so they can score well and pass without much reflexivity or critique.

Without critical thinking, students cannot engage and grow, and teachers cannot address controversial, judgemental or ethical concepts which require careful analysis. It takes years and decades to help students think in this way and to train them to develop their own understanding of any idea or concept. For example, the thousands of Chinese students who come to the United Kingdom to study for a master's degree really struggle to write critical essays, as at an undergraduate level, they have had no such training, and they find the English language a struggle as well. Entire education systems in many parts of the world would need to change if they are to empower people to think for themselves and articulate their own visions and values. The teaching of accounting and finance requires critical questioning and thinking for students to be able to exercise professional judgement.

The ideas in this book are very political, as they challenge the status quo and at the same time call for a revolution in the content and methods of education. Big business, big finance and big accounting firms are a problem to be discussed and not a formula to be celebrated and endorsed uncritically. Such a challenge can have direct implications on big endowments and on research grants and profiles. They may also impact student recruitment and elite rankings. Where pro-business scholarship is criticised, the academy is being asked to justify its knowledge base, relevance and social and environmental impact. As Said (1993) explained, all academic writing is political in its very nature and construction, and for academics to pretend not to have values or moral positions is to either lie or to mislead their students and readers. All intellectuals are of their time and place; the ivory tower simply does not exist. People cannot pretend to isolate themselves from the world, its institutions and dogmas. Intellectuals are part of the social world and cannot disengage from it.

Sustainability presents a significant challenge to contemporary business theory and practice, and this cannot be denied; otherwise, we are all sleepwalking into an abyss. There is a deliberate position taken in this book against mass and impersonal factory-style business education, and the greed of the business school or college to maximise profits. Viewed sustainably, educational establishments need to have a humane and responsible ethic (Shephard 2015), and practice the principles they preach in the way organisations respect knowledge, students and the physical and natural environment of learning. As an example, in the Indian tradition, wisdom and knowledge are attributed to a goddess called *Saraswati*, and she is worshipped by both students and teachers alike. The concept that teaching or research are sacred and divine roles in certain cultures is worthy of reflection.

In my personal experience, western business scholars and educators have significant cultural illiteracy, and this creates barriers for effective ethical business education. The fact that the English language is a dominant medium of discourse, both in the classroom and in textbooks and journals, creates huge barriers for other cultures and multi-cultural expression, including the introduction of different cultural theories of business. It has a significant impact on the classroom experience of students from diverse cultural backgrounds. It gives them the subliminal or often even direct impression that their culture, their history and experience is not worthy of study or reflection, and the only right way is the western 'scientific' way. This makes it very hard for students to even find the words and theories to have a serious intellectual dialogue about business ethics.

Teacher training about cultural intelligence and sensitivity is urgently needed in western business schools and all over the world. There is vast scientific evidence of unconscious bias when we meet people who are different from us, and this needs to be shown to business scholars to expose hidden prejudices and stereotypical views. Scholars also need to see how closed-minded they often are, as all too often they intellectualise about their open-mindedness, when they are truly not respectful of others. Lecturers should know that to convey a theory or concept effectively, they need to understand how different students will understand and translate their idea. It's about much more than language; it's about how they will perceive a theory depending on their own experiences and familiarities. A simple way out of this dilemma is to try to make the content acultural, but even then, there are problems with the understanding and interpretation as language is so deeply woven with culture. Also, all too often, the cultural assumptions behind the theories are hidden and suppressed, making the ideas partial and imposing rather than accessible and open to critique.

As scholars tend to be very protective of their thinking and theories, many would find the style and approach of this book very hard, as it can be perceived as an imposition of a particular ethic on them. They would not be used to being this personal about their values and belief or this passionate about a cause and its urgency. Western scientific culture is much more measured and sober, where emotions are meant to be regulated and rigorous theories and analysis are critical. Also, where scholars have spent their lives on the basis of particular assumptions about the world, about business, profit and wealth and about the possibilities of measurement and analysis, ideas about sustainability may prove very challenging for them. Most business school academics would see this book as too 'left wing' and too radical. However, even if we cannot change their mind-sets and baggage, we must endeavour to influence the young generation, as their very future is under threat. Also, many young people would be very receptive to such ideas and theories, as they too are concerned about the planet and its sustainability.

In a similar way, faith schools were and continue to be a huge influence on primary and secondary education all over the world. In fact, in some countries like India, the faith schools are often regarded as the best, and the Catholics all over the world are reputed for their educational standards and management. As we have already seen in business education, there is a denial of faith and a suppression of its influence on students and businesses.

This is not only untrue but also deeply damaging to ethical discourse because faith shows a sense of virtues and responsibility amongst its believers, and makes a very important starting point for ethical dialogue and study. To really transform global education on sustainable finance, we must engage directly with faith and definitely not deny its existence or importance.

It is, therefore, very likely that the lack of profound ethical engagement in both accounting and finance is deliberate. Science is being used as a deeply political weapon to authentify greed and exploitation as natural and the best way for business to operate or economies to run. The eminent scholar Bruno Latour (Latour 2014) sees economics and capitalism as a frontal attack on the environment and nature – a damaging weapon in the Anthropocene. The top journals of finance pretend to be totally apolitical and acultural, yet represent a prime example of greed, selfishness and unsustainable science. The knowledge factory in accounting and finance created in the West, with textbooks published by western-owned companies and PhDs awarded in the name of quality science and training, are highly suspect. They are disrespectful of the cultural diversity of the world, the fact that talent can come from anywhere and social sciences must be truly diverse in their theories and cultural assumptions. Modern economics eats culture for lunch and is a direct participant in our planetary destruction. Hence reform cannot come from tinkering at the margins of its science, where the critique has to be on its own terms and language.

Recent experience suggests that the more science is critiqued, the more inward mainstream finance and economics have become, demonstrating the huge power held by the intellectual elites in this field. There is an ideological war taking place, but the winners remain the old guard. One could also argue that big business does not want too many questions asked about its purpose and exploitative methods, and has captured the scientific process, directly and indirectly, to legitimate its actions. The Academy Award winning film *Inside Job* (Ferguson 2010) showed this beautifully in the context of the largest global financial crisis the world has ever experienced: the 2008 crash. Intellectuals were at the heart of its legitimation and continued to retain their jobs and professorial positions without any punishment or reprimand.

In recent years, there has been a massive process of internationalisation of business education, with many British and American Universities developing joint ventures abroad (see, e.g., Warwick 2014). These could be either with other Universities or opening their own campuses in foreign countries, trying to capitalise on their brand – a kind of education by profit-oriented, multi-national corporation. In the past, huge fees and profits were already being made by overseas students, who continue to finance a lot of western research. Now, more of these profits are being extracted at home without much change in the theories or methods. We need to look carefully at the content of their education syllabi and methods to see how truly multi-cultural it is, or whether this is a further step towards colonising world business education through greed and exploitation. The signs I have seen so far have not been very culture-sensitive, but more profit oriented and exploitative. As an example, in the United Kingdom, despite a huge international student cohort, there is not a single vice-chancellor of a major British University who is non-white today. The world is welcome to pay, but not to share; power and control in education needs to be white. If ethics must start from the inside out, then the teachers and systems of the western business schools cannot be ignored and must be transformed from within. We are still very far from that, in spite of the urgency of the ethical and environmental crises.

The cash cow that is business education today has bred a particular kind of culture, where exploitation of students and staff becomes the norm rather than the exception. In such an environment, we should not be surprised if the culture influences the behaviour of staff and the quality and content of their research and teaching curricula. In particular, such a culture would have a profound impact on the degree of challenge to big business and rich elites. Just as tax avoidance is exploitative of government funds and services, business schools are subtly endorsing a culture of enrichment and irresponsibility to society and the environment. The more the University relies on them as cash cows, the more this culture and abuse will become pervasive. The more aggressively we milk the cow, the sicker it becomes. In reforming education, the agenda is not simply about science and truth, but it is also about politics, culture and power. In such an atmosphere, the science and learning can easily be subverted, but we must try to resist this.

Fraud and corruption are common all over the world, and often business is at the heart of it. However, how they are implemented and by whom vary, but the classroom is a perfect place to discuss and analyse these facts. If research and material on this do not exist, the students could be involved in collecting the evidence, bringing newspaper cuttings and other facts, and they could then see how accounting and finance are not neutral, but often used to stretch the reality. Who has access to finance and investment and who does not is often a key factor in perpetuating inequality, but never discussed in the mainstream textbook.

The Arab Spring was started by a Tunisian street trader who set himself on fire in front of government offices when his vegetables and fruit scales were confiscated by the corrupt police. These were his entire life savings, and he was trying to make an honest living through hard work and thrift, something which is applauded in all business courses. However, the reality proved otherwise, and the government stopped him from making his own profits. Even though he had no access to finance, through hard work, he saved enough to buy the street cart, the scales and the stock of fruits and vegetables. This is the entrepreneurial spirit that exists all over the world. However, it was all taken away by the corrupt police for no reason at all, and he decided to set fire to himself in public as a frustrated person wanting to make a political point.

This small example could spark a significant discussion in class about power, finance, politics and enterprise, which may become etched in the student memories for a long time to come. Ethics can be powerfully conveyed in the form of stories, and local stories make them very highly relatable and understandable. They also unearth local facts about how business is practiced, who controls and what freedoms exist. Professionals can play an influential role in changing local practices and helping to bring about fairness and equity in such circumstances. As an example, they play a key role in helping small businesses raise finance. Once again, this fact is not discussed in corporate finance textbooks.

There are also significant global influences on local practices. For example, there are international accounting standards which apply to many large businesses all over the world. Tax is a major influence on accounting practices all over the world, though rarely discussed in the mainstream textbooks. In truth, tax also influences business location, transfer pricing, movement of finance and capital, and the offshore secrecy jurisdictions give huge opportunity for any business to hide their true profits and financial transactions from public view anywhere in the world. These go completely against the grain of accounting theory and standards, as well as finance theory. Corporate aims now are to avoid transparency and equality, and to practice fraud and corruption (Whyte and Wiegratz 2016). Every year, billions of dollars are hidden in this way by businesses from all over the world, having a significant impact on local and global economies. Accounting practices are key to tax avoidance, and this needs to be discussed in the classroom. Similarly, the role of professional accountants and bankers in helping their clients minimise tax has significant ethical implications which can also be discussed and debated.

Unfortunately, the factory model of teaching is very common in many parts of the world, making it very difficult to make education personal. This also makes it impossible to enable students to think for themselves and help them in cultivating their own values and judgements. The idea of students doing their own research and uncovering local practices and stories is anathema. The teacher is the expert, and the sole focus is to pass exams and do well so that one can get a job at the end. The best teachers are ones who get the best exam results, and the best students are ones who can memorise and implement the rules and techniques to pass the exams.

In such an environment, even trying to understand and challenge the DNA of business, or its wider social and environmental impact, becomes significantly challenging. In fact, even in the West, a lot of accounting and finance programmes are hugely profitable to Universities and, therefore, taught in a factory format to maximise profits. Despite a culture of challenge and critique, this is not facilitated. The best example of this is when economics students at the world famous University of Manchester rebelled collectively against their narrow and technocratic teaching curriculum (PCES 2014). The University took six months to consider their complaints and then decided to virtually change nothing. This is the reality of the hold on the discipline by the experts and by research funders and rankings. The truth is set aside in the pursuit of complexity and prestige.

Field trips are a very important way to learn about local business practices and their social and environmental impacts. They also help students to connect deeply with one another and to socialise and personalise their learning journey. They can help them in uncovering stories and examples from their own experience which they never thought would be relevant in the classroom. When students go away, they learn the wider context of business, its real-world compromises and customs, and discover in the stories of small businesses the huge personal sacrifices and efforts people make to serve and make a living. Here accounting and finance may not be very complex, but they certainly will be very real. Small businesses need to count and control every penny, and often operate without formal business or accountancy training. The question students could ask them is how do they cope and to those businesses which have grown, what kind of business training they actually received and where do they go to for knowledge and advice.

In the first-year freshers week of my undergraduate class, I decided to take students to a local accounting firm called Ensors, where trainees presented their experiences of working there. I was surprised to discover that some of my students had never entered a professional office before and were really awed by the icebreaking experience. One decided that he is no longer going to be small entrepreneur, but a professional person who can help others to grow and build their businesses. This small example conveys how powerful it can be to facilitate such experiences and give students the opportunity to actually meet local firms and businesses and learn how they operate from the inside. For the teacher, organising this may be demanding on time and resources, but this should not become an excuse. In my experience, local businesses can be very helpful and obliging, and actually love the opportunity to engage with students and share their stories.

Local history, politics, culture, law and networks all matter in the practice of business. Not all of these facts and influences would be recorded in global textbooks; in fact, they are often ignored completely where the content is purely technical (see e.g. Deegan and Ward 2013). In many countries of the world, networks are the key to making things happen, and skill and business acumen do not count much, but who you know does. In other countries, technology and social media can help shape the networks and promote the products one wishes to sell. Similarly, in professional practice, networks play a huge role in getting clients and helping clients to raise finance or obtain advice and resources to grow and nurture fledgling enterprises. Students could study how these networks are built and what role faith and community groupings play in building trust and camaraderie. In this way, they will begin to see the role of social capital in business and finance, and how it can be nurtured and harnessed. None of this would be explained in the global accounting and finance textbooks, which, by their very construction, can only be formulaic.

Mapping is a visual tool of making power, culture, politics and networks visible and analysable. Students could be asked to undertake such local mapping exercises as homework for their class, and in this way, local research can be compiled. They may discover really good entrepreneurs who are able to leverage these factors to their advantage and share their stories openly. Some of them may even offer to mentor students on their learning journey, which could be very beneficial to them. It helps them see that there are people who care for young students and their careers, and are willing to share their skills and experience for free. Some of them may even share their contacts to help them find a job or get good quality internships and training. The glamour of success that is often attached to business, finance and entrepreneurship can be unveiled by the reality of risk and experience.

History is rarely discussed in journals and books on business ethics, giving the impression that the past is not relevant to understanding business and its conduct and influence. Even Craig and Matten (2010) write as if business ethics were a new invention. Modernity and technology tends to make the past backward and irrelevant, but this could not be far from the truth. History also is a very helpful way of showing context and enables students to see the wide range of factors which influence business success, not just the entrepreneur. It can help them step out of the bubble that is accounting and finance. The past has always had some influence on the present and can enrich our understanding of what and how things and organisations truly endure. Hopefully, in this way, students will discover that ethics and virtues are the only qualities sustainable in life – all else comes and goes, as death is a certainty. This could be very empowering and potentially liberating for them.

Influences on business practice in different parts of the world could range from the legal system, the social capital, family values and trust, property ownership and rights and even the role of governments and elites in supporting or inhibiting business growth. True-life stories of businesses or successful business families could illuminate local factors which collectively influence business success. Students from that country would be able to relate to these stories much better and even become empowered to ask questions. Where businesses have failed, they could understand the factors which make them unsustainable and how future organisations could be kept solvent and sustainable. The examples may even reveal to them that wealth is not always the key to happiness and that it can give rise to much conflict and strife in the family. Students could be asked to dig out their own family histories if there have been business start-ups and share the experiences of these over the years. I know my community is full of these stories.

Teacher training is key to building quality student experiences and sharing best practice and building sustainable education. The absence of this despite the huge demand for accounting and finance education is very disturbing. If we are keen to build a sustainable planet, then resources must be put in this area, especially in parts of the world where there are no established Universities or research and mentoring networks. Private colleges may provide a better education due to the market discipline they follow, but rarely invest in the research and training required to sustain this and to innovate. Many of them can probably afford to set money and resources aside for this, but are short termist and greedy in their orientation. This is sad and regressive. Given the personal approach adopted in this book, it must be recognised that teachers and lecturers are also human beings, and they need to be respected and valued as such. The culture of the college or University also has a big influence on how ethical teaching is delivered and the way in which it transforms the students, or fails to do so.

Bibliography

AACSB (2016) *A Collective Vision for Business Education*, Tampa, FL: AACSB, www.aacsb.edu

Admati, A. and Hellwig, M. (2013) *The Bankers New Clothes*, Princeton: Princeton University Press.

Angelides, P. et al. (2011) 'The Financial Crisis Inquiry Report', *Financial Crisis Inquiry Commission*, New York, p. 633.

Armstrong, K. (2006) *The Great Transformation: The World in the Time of Buddha, Socrates, Confucius and Jeremiah*, London: Atlantic Books.

Arnold, P. (2009) Global financial crisis: The challenge to accounting research, *Accounting, Organisations and Society*, 34, pp. 803–809.

Arnold, P. (2012) The political economy of financial harmonisation: The East Asian financial crisis and the rise of international accounting standards, *Accounting, Organisations & Society*, 37, pp. 361–381.

Bakan, J. (2004) *The Corporation: The Pathological Pursuit of Profit and Power*, New York: Free Press.

Balakrishnan, J., Malhotra, A. and Falkenberg, L. (2017) Multi-level corporate responsibility – a comparison of Gandhi's trusteeship with stakeholder and stewardship frameworks, *Journal of Business Ethics*, 141, pp. 133–150.

Beck, U. (1992) *Risk Society: Towards a New Modernity*, London: Sage Publications.

Bentley-Hart, D. (2013) *The Experience of God – Being, Consciousness, and Bliss*, New Haven: Yale University Press.

Boatright, J. (1999) *Ethics in Finance*, Oxford: Blackwell.

Brealey, R., Myers, S. and Allen, F. (2014) *Principles of Corporate Finance*, 11th Edition, New York: McGraw-Hill.

Broadbent, J. and Laughlin, R. (2013) *Accounting Control and Controlling Accounting – Interdisciplinary and Critical Perspectives*, Bingley, UK: Emerald.

Brooks, R. (2014) *The Great Tax Robbery*, London: One World.

Cassidy, J. (2002) *Dot Con: The Greatest Story Ever Told*, New York: Harper Collins.

Chabrak, N. and Craig, R. (2013) Student imaginings, cognitive dissonance and critical thinking, *Critical Perspectives on Accounting*, 24:2, pp. 91–104.

Chang, H. J. (2010) *23 Things They Don't Tell You about Capitalism*, London: Bloomsbury.

Chang, H. J. and Aldred, J. (2014) After the crash, we need a revolution in the way we teach economics, *The Guardian*, 11 May.

Coggan, P. (2012) *Paper Promises: Money, Debt and the New World Order*, Harmondsworth: Penguin.

Cohan, W. (2011) *Money and Power: How Goldman Sachs Came to Rule the World*, New York: Penguin.

Cooper, D., Everett, J. and Neu, D. (2005) Financial scandals, accounting change and the role of accounting academics: A perspective from North America, *European Accounting Review*, 14:2, pp. 373–382.

Crane, A. and Matten, D. (2010) *Business Ethics, 3rd edition*. Oxford: Oxford University Press.

Daly, H. and Cobb, J. (1994) *For the Common Good: Redirecting the Economy toward Community, Environment and a Sustainable Future*, 2nd Edition, Boston: Beacon Press.

Das, S. (2011) *Extreme Money: The Masters of the Universe and the Cult of Risk*, New York: Financial Times Series.

Deegan, C. and Ward, A. (2013) *Financial Accounting and Reporting: An International Approach*, London: McGraw-Hill.

Dixson, A. and Rousseau, C. (2006) *Critical Race Theory in Education*, London: Routledge.

Donaldson, P. (1984) *Economics of the Real World*, 3rd Edition, London: Penguin.

Douglas, M. and Wildavsky, A. (1982) *Risk and Culture*, Berkeley, CA: University of California Press.

Economist (2015) Going global – secrets of the world's best business people, 16 December, www.economist.com

Edwards, J. and Walker, S. (2009) *The Routledge Companion to Accounting History*, London: Routledge.

Ekins, P., Hillman, M. and Hutchison, R. (1992) *Wealth Beyond Measure: An Atlas of New Economics*, London: Gaia Books.

Elkington, J. (1999) *Cannibals with Forks: The Triple Bottom Line of 21st Century Business*, Oxford: Capstone.

Engelen, E., Erturk, I., Froud, J., Johal, S., Leaver, A., Moran, M. and Williams, K. (2012) Misrule of experts? The financial crisis as elite debacle, *Economy and Society*, 41:3, pp. 360–382.

Erturk, I., Froud, J., Johal, S., Leaver, A. and Williams, K. (2007) Against agency: A positional critique, *Economy and Society*, 36, pp. 51–77.

Erturk, I., Froud, J., Johal, S., Leaver, A. and Williams, K. (2008) *Financialisation at Work*, London: Routledge.

Ferguson, C. (2010) *Inside Job*, Feature Documentary on the 2008 Crash, Director: Charles Ferguson, 108 minutes, USA.

Ferguson, C. (2012) *Inside Job: The Financiers Who Pulled off the Heist of the Century*, London: One World.

Ferguson, J., Collinson, D., Power, D. and Stevenson, L. (2009) Constructing meaning in the service of power: An analysis of the typical modes of ideology in accounting textbooks, *Critical Perspectives on Accounting*, 20:8, pp. 896–909.

Ferguson, N. (2012) *The Ascent of Money: A Financial History of the World*, Harmondsworth: Penguin.

Financial Inclusion Commission (2015) *Financial Inclusion: Improving the Financial Health of a Nation*, London: Financial Inclusion Commission.

Finel-Honigman, I. (2010) *A Cultural History of Finance*, London: Routledge.

Fleming, P. and Jones, M. (2012) *The End of Corporate Social Responsibility: Crisis and Critique*, London: Sage Publications.

Frankfurter, G. and McGoun, E. (2002) *From Individualism to the Individual: Ideology and Inquiry in Financial Economics*, Farnham: Ashgate.

Fraser, I. (2015) *Shredded: Inside RBS – the Bank That Broke Britain*, Edinburgh: Birlinn.

Froud, J., Johal, S., Leaver, A. and Williams, K. (2006) *Financialisation and Strategy: Narrative and Numbers*, London: Routledge.

Gambling Commission (2017) *Gambling Participation in 2016 – Behaviour, Awareness and Attitudes*, Annual Report, February, Birmingham, UK: Gambling Commission

Gendron, Y. (2013) Accounting academia and the threat of the paying off mentality, *Critical Perspectives on Accounting*, 26, pp. 168–176.

Gendron, Y. and Smith-Lacroix, J. (2013) The global financial crisis: Essay on the possibility of substantive change in the discipline of finance, *Critical Perspectives on Accounting*, 30, pp. 83–101.

Gentile, M. (2011) A faculty forum on *giving voice to values* – faculty perspectives on the uses of this pedagogy and curriculum for values-driven leadership, *Journal of Business Ethics Education*, 8, pp. 305–307.

Germain, R. (2010) *Global Politics and Financial Governance*, London: Palgrave Macmillan.

Graeber, D. (2014) *Debt: The First 5000 Years*, Brooklyn, NY: Melville House.

Graham, C. (2013) Teaching accounting as a language, *Critical Perspectives on Accounting*, 24, pp. 120–126.

Gray, R. and Bebbington, J. (2001) *Accounting for the Environment*, 2nd Edition, London: Sage Publications.

Hanlon, G. (1994) *The Commercialisation of Accountancy*, London: Macmillan Press.

Hare, R. D. (1996) *Without Conscience: The Disturbing World of the Psychopaths among Us*, New York: The Guilford Press.

Harney, S. and Dunne, S. (2013) More than nothing? Accounting, business and management studies and the research audit, *Critical Perspectives on Accounting*, 24, pp. 338–349.

Hawken, P. (1994) *The Ecology of Commerce: A Declaration of Sustainability*, London: Phoenix.

HBR (2016) *On Managing across Cultures*, Boston: Harvard Business Review Press.

Heffernan, M. (2011) *Wilful Blindness: Why We Ignore the Obvious at Our Peril*, New York: Walker & Co.

Hendry, J. (2013) *Ethics and Finance: An Introduction*, Cambridge: Cambridge University Press.

Hertz, N. (2001) *The Silent Takeover: Global Capitalism and the Death of Democracy*, London: William Heinemann.

Hightower, J. (2004) *Thieves in High Places*, New York: Penguin Books.

Hirsch, F. (1976) *The Social Limits to Growth*, Cambridge, MA: Harvard University Press.

Holland, D. and Albrecht, C. (2013) The worldwide academic field of business ethics: Scholars perceptions of the most important issues, *Journal of Business Ethics*, 117, pp. 777–788.

Hopper, T. (2013) Making accounting degrees fit for a university, *Critical Perspectives on Accounting*, 24:2, pp. 127–135.

Hopwood, A. (2007) Whither accounting research?, *The Accounting Review*, 82:5, pp. 1365–1374.

Hopwood, A. (2008) Changing pressures on the research process: On trying to research in an age when curiosity in not enough, *European Accounting Review*, 17:1, pp. 87–96.

Hopwood, A. (2009) Exploring the interface between accounting and finance, *Accounting, Organisations and Society*, 34, pp. 549–550.

Kamla, R. (2015) Critical Muslim intellectuals thought: Possible contributions to the development of emancipatory accounting thought, *Critical Perspectives on Accounting*, 31, pp. 64–74.

Kay, J. (2011) The map is not the territory: an essay on the state of economics, *Institute for New Economic Thinking* (blog). Retrieved from http://ineteconomics.org/blog/inet/john-kay-map-not-territory-essay-state-eceonomics

Kay, J. (2015) *Other People's Money: Masters of the Universe or Servants of the People?*, London: Profile Books.

Kets de Vries, M. (2012) *The Psychopath in the C Suite: Redefining the SOB*, Insead Working Paper No. 19.

Kim, S. (2013) Reforming the business school, a pure product of American culture, *Huffington Post*, 24 September.

Klein, N. (2007) *The Shock Doctrine – the Rise of Disaster Capitalism*, London: Penguin Books.

Korten, D. C. (1995) *When Corporations Rule the World*, London: Earthscan.

Lail, B., MacGregor, J., Marcum, M. and Stuebs, M. (2017) Virtuous professionalism in accountants to avoid fraud and to restore financial reporting, *Journal of Business Ethics*, 140, pp. 687–704.

Latour, B. (2014) *On Some of the Affects of Capitalism*, Copenhagen: Royal Academy.

Lehman, C. R. (2013) Knowing the unknowable and contested terrains in accounting, *Critical Perspectives on Accounting*, 24, pp. 136–144.

Lewis, M. (2008) *The Big Short*, London: Penguin Publishing.

Lewis, M. (2011) *Boomerang: The Biggest Bust*, London: Penguin Books.

Loeb, S. (2015) Active learning – an advantageous yet challenging approach to accounting ethics education, *Journal of Business Ethics*, 127, pp. 221–230.

Luyendijk, J. (2015) *Swimming with Sharks: My Journey into the World of Bankers*, London: Guardian/Faber&Faber.

Mackenzie, D. (2006) *An Engine, Not a Camera: How Financial Models Shape Markets*, Cambridge, MA: MIT Press.

McBarnet, D. and Whelan, C. (1992) 'International corporate finance and the challenge of creative compliance', in Fingleton, J. (Ed.) *The Internationalisation of*

Capital Markets and the Regulatory Response, London: Graham & Trotman, pp. 129–142.

McBarnet, D. and Whelan, C. (1999) *Creative Accounting and the Cross-Eyed Javelin Thrower*, Chichester, UK: Wiley.

McDonald, L. and Robinson, P. (2009) *A Colossal Failure of Common Sense: The Incredible Inside Story of the Collapse of Lehman Brothers*, London: Ebury Press.

McFall, J. et al. (2009) 'Banking Crisis: Reforming Corporate Governance and the City', House of Commons Treasury Committee, HC 519.

McGoun, E. (1997) Hyperreal finance, *Critical Perspectives on Accounting*, 18, pp. 97–122.

McGoun, E. and Zielonka, P. (2006) The platonic foundations of finance and the interpretation of finance models, *Journal of Behavioral Finance*, 7:1, pp. 43–57.

McKernan, J. F. (2011) Deconstruction and the responsibilities of the accounting academic, *Critical Perspectives on Accounting*, 22, pp. 698–713.

McPhail, K. and Ferguson, J. (2016) The past, the present and the future of accounting for human rights, *Accounting, Auditing and Accountability Journal*, 29, pp. 526–541.

McPhail, K. and Walters, D. (2009) *Accounting and Business Ethics: An Introduction*, London: Routledge.

McSweeney, B. (2009) The roles of financial asset market failure denial and the economic crisis: Reflections on accounting and financial theories and practices, *Accounting, Organisations & Society*, 34, pp. 835–848.

Mele, D., Rosanas, J. and Fontrodona, J. (2016) Ethics in finance and accounting – an introduction, *Journal of Business Ethics*, 140, pp. 609–613.

Mitchell, A. and Sikka, P. (2011) *The Pin-Stripe Mafia: How Accountancy Firms Destroy Societies*, London: Association for Accountancy & Business Affairs.

Molisa, P. (2011) A spiritual reflection on emancipation and accounting, *Critical Perspectives on Accounting*, 22, pp. 453–484.

Monbiot, G. (2000) *The Corporate Takeover of Britain*, London: Macmillan.

Moore, M. (2001) *Stupid White Men*, London: Penguin.

Murphy, R. (2015) *The Joy of Tax*, London: Transworld Publishers.

Nordenflycht, A. (2010) What is a professional service firm – toward a theory and taxonomy of knowledge intensive firms, *Academy of Management Review*, 35:1, pp. 155–174.

Oates, G. and Dias, R. (2016) Including ethics in banking and finance programs – teaching 'we shouldn't win at any cost', *Education + Training*, 58:1, pp. 94–111.

Palan, R., Murphy, R. and Chavagneux, C. (2010) *How Globalisation Really Works*, Ithaca, NY: Cornell University Press.

Parker, L. and Guthrie, J. (2014) Addressing directions in interdisciplinary accounting research, *Accounting, Auditing and Accountability Journal*, 27:8, pp. 1218–1226.

PCES (2014) *Economics, Education and Unlearning, Post-Crash Economics Society*, Manchester: University of Manchester Press.

Pehlivanova, P. and Martinoff, M. (2015) *Philosophy for Accountancy*, London: ICAEW – Audit Futures.

Peston, R. (2008) *Who Runs Britain? . . . And Who's to Blame for the Economic Mess We're in*, London: Hodder & Stoughton.

Pettigrew, A. and Starkey, K. (2016) The legitimacy and impact of business schools – key issues and a research agenda, *Academy of Management Learning and Education*, 15:4, pp. 649–664.

Pfeffer, J. and Fong, C. (2002) The end of business schools? Less success than meets the eye, *Academy of Management Learning and Education*, 1:1, pp. 78–95.

Picciotto, S. (2007) Constructing compliance: Game playing, tax law and the regulatory state, *Law & Policy*, 29:1, January, pp. 11–29.

Picciotto, S. (2015) Indeterminacy, complexity, technocracy and the reform of international corporate taxation, *Social & Legal Studies*, 24:2, pp. 165–184.

Power, M. (2007) *Organised Uncertainty: Designing a World of Risk Management*, Oxford: Oxford University Press.

Rajan, R. and Zingales, L. (2003) *Saving Capitalism from the Capitalists*, New York: Crown Business.

Rand, A. (1957) *Atlas Shrugged*, New York: Random House.

Rebele, J. and St. Pierre, E. (2015) Stagnation in accounting education research, *Journal of Accounting Education*, 33, pp. 128–137.

Ross, S., Westerfield, R. and Jordan, B. (2012) *Fundamentals of Corporate Finance*, 9th Edition, New York: McGraw-Hill International Edition.

Ruskin, J. (1862) *Unto This Last and Other Writings*, London: Penguin Classics.

Said, E. (1993) *BBC Reith Lectures 1993: Representations of the Intellectual*, London: British Broadcasting Corporation.

Said, E. (1994) *Culture and Imperialism*, London: Vintage Books.

Santoro, M. and Strauss, R. (2013) *Wall Street Values*, New York: Cambridge University Press.

Sayer, A. (2016) 'Moral economy, unearned income and legalized corruption', in Whyte, D. and Wigratz, J. (Eds.) *Neoliberalism and the Moral Economy of Fraud*, London: Routledge, pp. 44–56.

Seto-Pamies, D. and Papaoikonomou, E. (2016) A multi-level perspective for the integration of Ethics, Corporate Social Responsibility and Sustainability (ECSRS) in management education, *Journal of Business Ethics*, 136, pp. 523–538.

Shah, A. (1996a) Corporate governance and business ethics, *Business Ethics: A European Review*, 5:4, pp. 225–233.

Shah, A. (1996b) Creative compliance in financial reporting, *Accounting, Organisations and Society*, 21:1, pp. 23–39.

Shah, A. (1997a) Regulatory arbitrage through financial innovation, *Accounting, Auditing and Accountability Journal*, 10:1, pp. 85–104.

Shah, A. (1997b) The social dimensions of financial risk, *Journal of Financial Regulation and Compliance*, September, pp. 195–207.

Shah, A. (2007) *Celebrating Diversity: How to Enjoy, Respect and Benefit from Great Coloured Britain*, Buxhall, UK: Kevin Mayhew.

Shah, A. (2014) Drugs and the City: An Open Secret, So Why No Testing?, www.theconversation.com

Shah, A. (2015a) *The Political Economy of Financial Risk – a Case Study of HBOS*, Working Paper, www.academia.edu

Shah, A. (2015b) *Systemic Regulatory Arbitrage – a Case Study of KPMG*, Working Paper, www.academia.edu

Shah, A. (2016) Q. What did universities learn from the financial crash? A. Nothing, *The Guardian*, 2 February, www.guardian.co.uk

Shah, A. (2017) *The Politics of Risk, Audit and Regulation: A Case Study of HBOS*, London: Routledge.

Shah, A. and Rankin, A. (2017) *Jainism and Ethical Finance*, London: Routledge.

Shaxson, N. (2012) *Treasure Islands: Tax Havens and the Men Who Stole the World*, London: Vintage Books.

Shaxson, N. and Christensen, J. (2013) The finance curse, *Tax Justice Network*, p. 89. Retrieved from taxjustice.net/cms/upload/pdf/Finance_Curse_Final.pdf

Shefrin, H. (2000) *Beyond Greed and Fear: Understanding Behavioural Finance and the Psychology of Investing*, Cambridge, MA: Harvard Business School Press.

Shephard, K. (2015) *Higher Education for Sustainable Development*, London: Palgrave Macmillan.

Shiller, R. J. (2012) *Finance and the Good Society*, Princeton: Princeton University Press.

Sikka, P. (2008) Enterprise culture and accountancy firms: New masters of the universe, *Accounting, Auditing and Accountability Journal*, 21:2, pp. 268–295.

Sikka, P., Willmott, H. and Puxty, T. (1995) The mountains are still there – accounting academics and the bearings of intellectuals, *Accounting, Auditing & Accountability Journal*, 8:3, pp. 113–140.

Stout, D. (2016) Things I have learned (thus far) . . . reflections of an accounting academic, *Journal of Accounting Education*, 35, pp. 1–19.

Strange, S. (1986) *Casino Capitalism*, Oxford: Basil Blackwell.

Subcommittee on Investigations (2011) *Wall Street and the Financial Crisis: Anatomy of a Financial Collapse*, Washington, DC: Unites States Senate Permanent Committee on Investigations.

Tax Justice Network (2015) *The Greatest Invention: Tax and the Campaign for a Just Society*, London: Commonwealth Publishing.

Tett, G. (2010) *Fool's Gold: How Unrestrained Greed Corrupted a Dream, Shattered Global Markets and Unleashed a Catastrophe*, London: Abacus.

Tett, G. (2015) *The Silo Effect: The Peril of Expertise and the Promise of Breaking Down Barriers*, New York: Simon & Shuster.

Tweedie, D., Dyball, M., Hazelton, J. and Wright, S. (2013) Teaching global ethical standards – a case and strategy for broadening the accounting ethics curriculum, *Journal of Business Ethics*, 115, pp. 1–15.

Tyrie, A. et al. (2013) *Changing Banking for Good*, London: House of Commons Treasury Committee Report HC175–11.

Unerman, J., Bebbington, J. and O'Dwyer, B. (2007) *Sustainaibility Accounting and Accountability*, London: Routledge.

Wachtel, P. (1983) *The Poverty of Affluence: A Psychological Portrait of the American Way of Life*, New York: Free Press.

Warwick, P. (2014) The international business of higher education – a managerial perspective on the internationalisation of UK universities, *International Journal of Management Education*, 12:2, pp. 91–103.

West, B. (2003) *Professionalism and Accounting Rules*, London: Routledge.

West, J. (2015) Quantitative method in finance: From detachment to ethical engagement. *Journal of Business Ethics*, *129*, 599–611. doi:10.1007/s10551-014-2193-9

Whyte, D. and Wiegratz, J. (Eds.) (2016) *Neoliberalism and the Moral Economy of Fraud*, London: Routledge.

Willmott, H. (2011) Journal list fetishism and the perversion of scholarship: Reactivity and the ABS list, *Organisation*, 18:4, pp. 429–442.

Zeff, S. A. (1995) David Solomons (1912–1995) – an appreciation, *Accounting and Business Research*, Autumn, pp. 315–319.

Zwan, N. (2014) Making sense of financialisation, *Socio-Economic Review*, 12, pp. 99–129.

Index

Printed in the United States
by Baker & Taylor Publisher Services